HOW TO DRAW PEOPLE

USING THE MAGIC OF LINE

By Anna Nadler

Copyright © 2022 Anna Nadler
All rights reserved
Published by Anna Nadler Art
No part of this publication may be
reproduced, stored in a retrieval system or
transmitted in any form or by any means,
electronic, mechanical, photocopying, recording
or otherwise, without prior written permission
from the author/publisher.
www.annanadlerart.com

ISBN: 978-1-958428-14-6

Table of Contents

p.4-5 - About the author

p.6 - Introduction

p.7-9 - The skeleton

p.10-11 - Stick figure and practice page

p.12-13 - Drawing action and practice page

p.14-15 - Seated pose and practice page

p.16-17 - Walking pose and practice page

p.18-19 - Running pose and practice page

p.20-21 - Head and face and practice page

p.22-23 - Head views and practice page

p.24-25 - Right and wrong way to draw hair

p.26-27 - Hair drawing examples and practice

p.28-29 - Drawing stylized people and practice

p.30-31 - Drawing eyes and practice page

Table of Contents

p.32-33 - Drawing noses and practice page

p.34-35 - Drawing lips and practice page

p.36-37 - Drawing ears and practice page

p.38-39 - Drawing a hand and practice page

p.40-41 - Hand positions and practice page

p.42-43 - Drawing feet and practice page

p.44-45 - Drawing kids vs. adults and practice

p.46-47 - Drawing clothing and practice page

p.48-49 - Drawing back views and practice

p.50-51 - Drawing tricky body positions

p.52-53 - How to get a likeness of a person?

p.54 - Let's celebrate our differences

p.55 - Portrait practice instructions

p.56-57 - Final note

p.58-59 - Collect all of our"how to" books

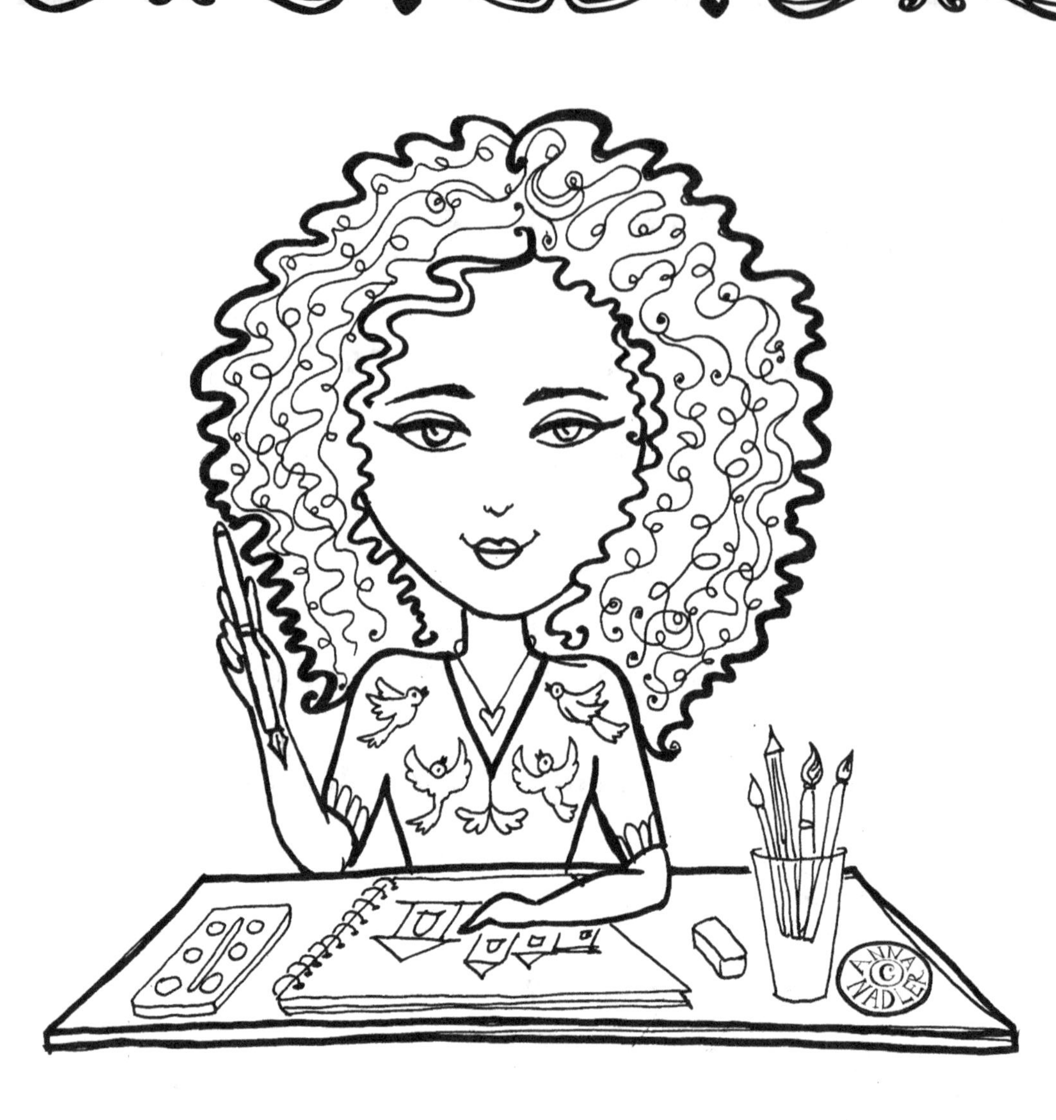

Anna Nadler is a book illustrator who
lives and works in New York City.
She has been drawing since the age of
two - it's been her life-long passion
and career for several decades.
Anna has taught both kids and adults
how to draw, and has finally decided
to put some of that knowledge into
a simple and comprehensive book
for everyone to benefit.

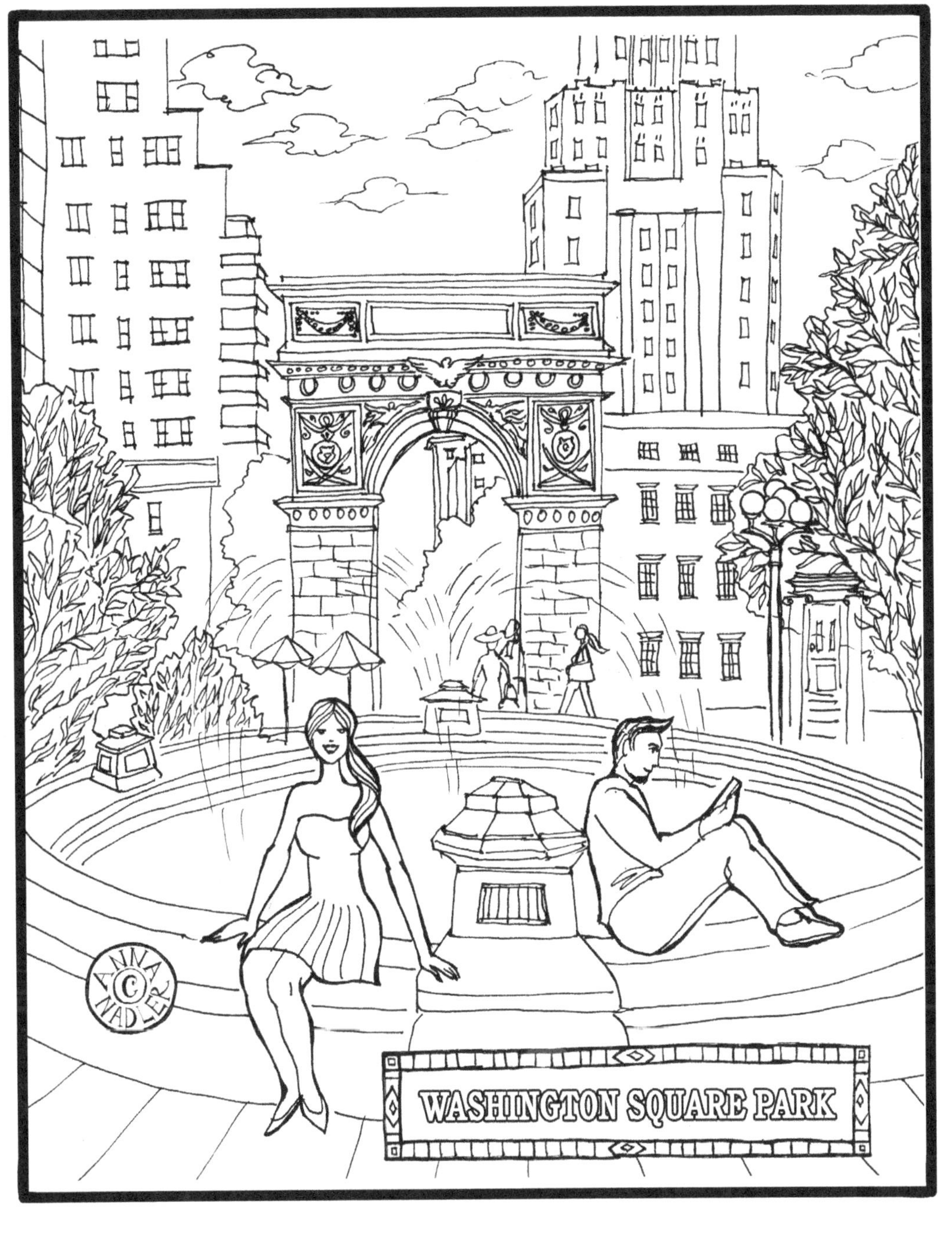

Anna has a special passion for drawing
people and places; she goes out to draw
from life any chance she gets.
You can find many of her coloring books,
children's books, activity books,
and more online and in stores.

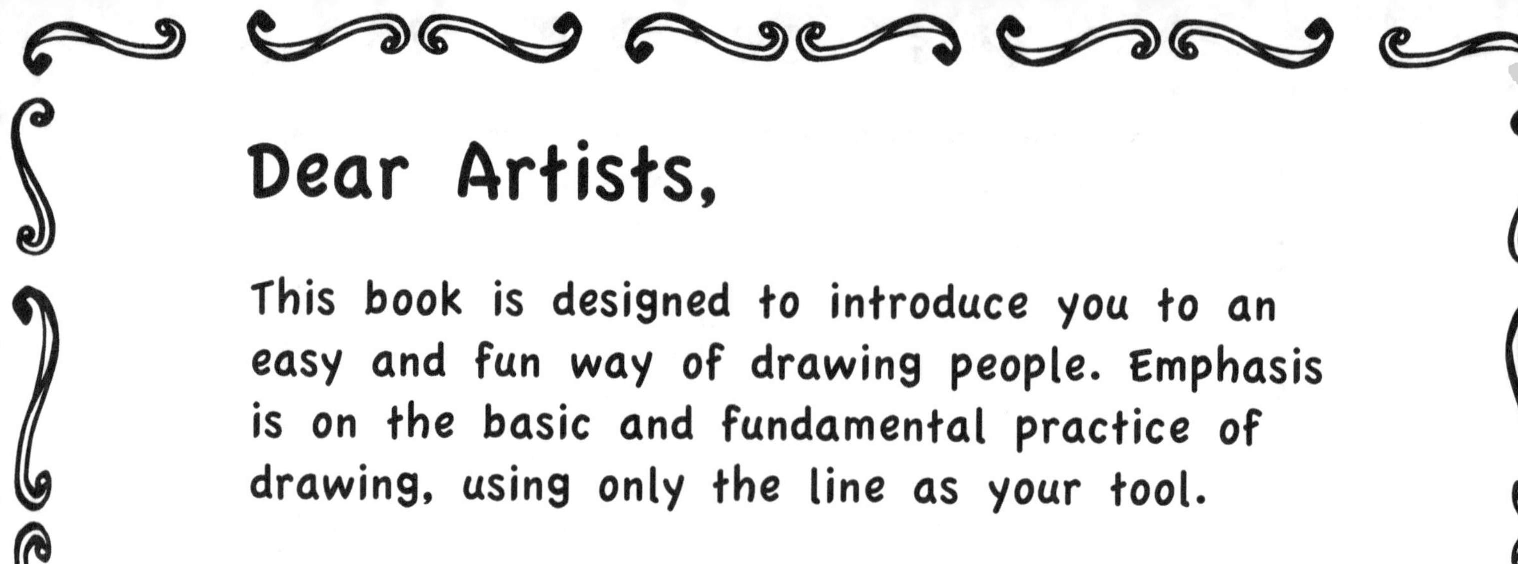

Dear Artists,

This book is designed to introduce you to an easy and fun way of drawing people. Emphasis is on the basic and fundamental practice of drawing, using only the line as your tool.

This book does not cover any rendering, shading or crosshatching techniques. Before you get into any of those, you need to know how to draw the body well.

In fact, if you can draw people well, you will be able to show all you need with a few simple but expressive lines, like many great illustrators of the past, such as Al Herschfeld and Shel Silverstein.

Drawing people can be intimidating, but it doesn't have to be. By following a few simple rules, which you can universally apply to your cartoons, portraits and sketches of people, you will enjoy the process and will come up with great & creative drawings of people!

Feel free to color in your drawings with color pencils whenever you feel the urge to. Simple tonal color will suffice.

So sit back, relax, and enjoy this book!

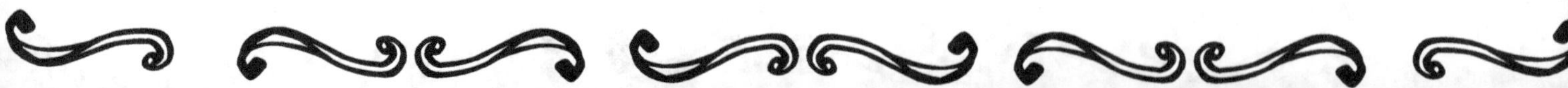

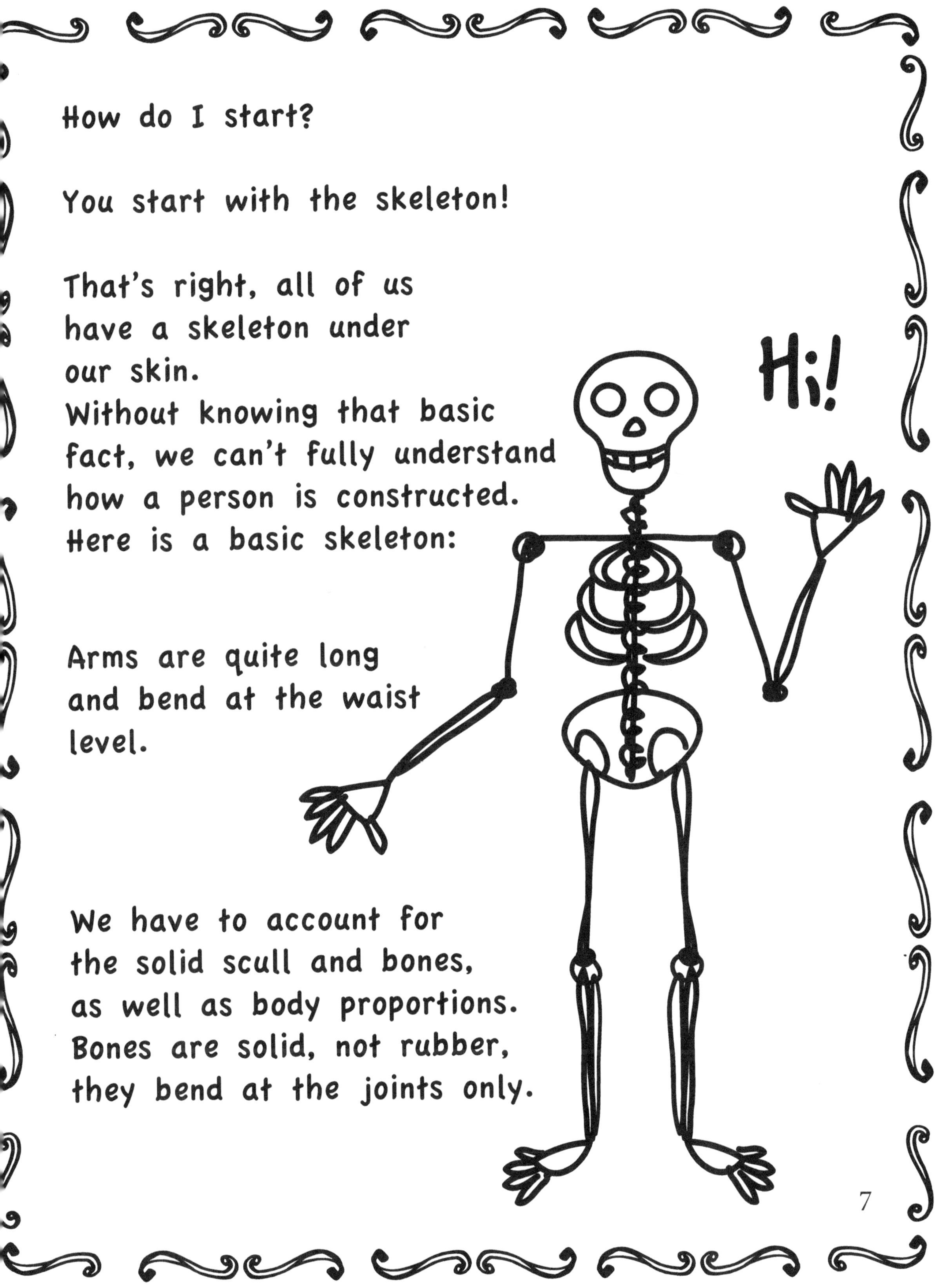

How do I start?

You start with the skeleton!

That's right, all of us
have a skeleton under
our skin.
Without knowing that basic
fact, we can't fully understand
how a person is constructed.
Here is a basic skeleton:

Arms are quite long
and bend at the waist
level.

We have to account for
the solid scull and bones,
as well as body proportions.
Bones are solid, not rubber,
they bend at the joints only.

On top of the skeleton are muscles and then skin and hair.

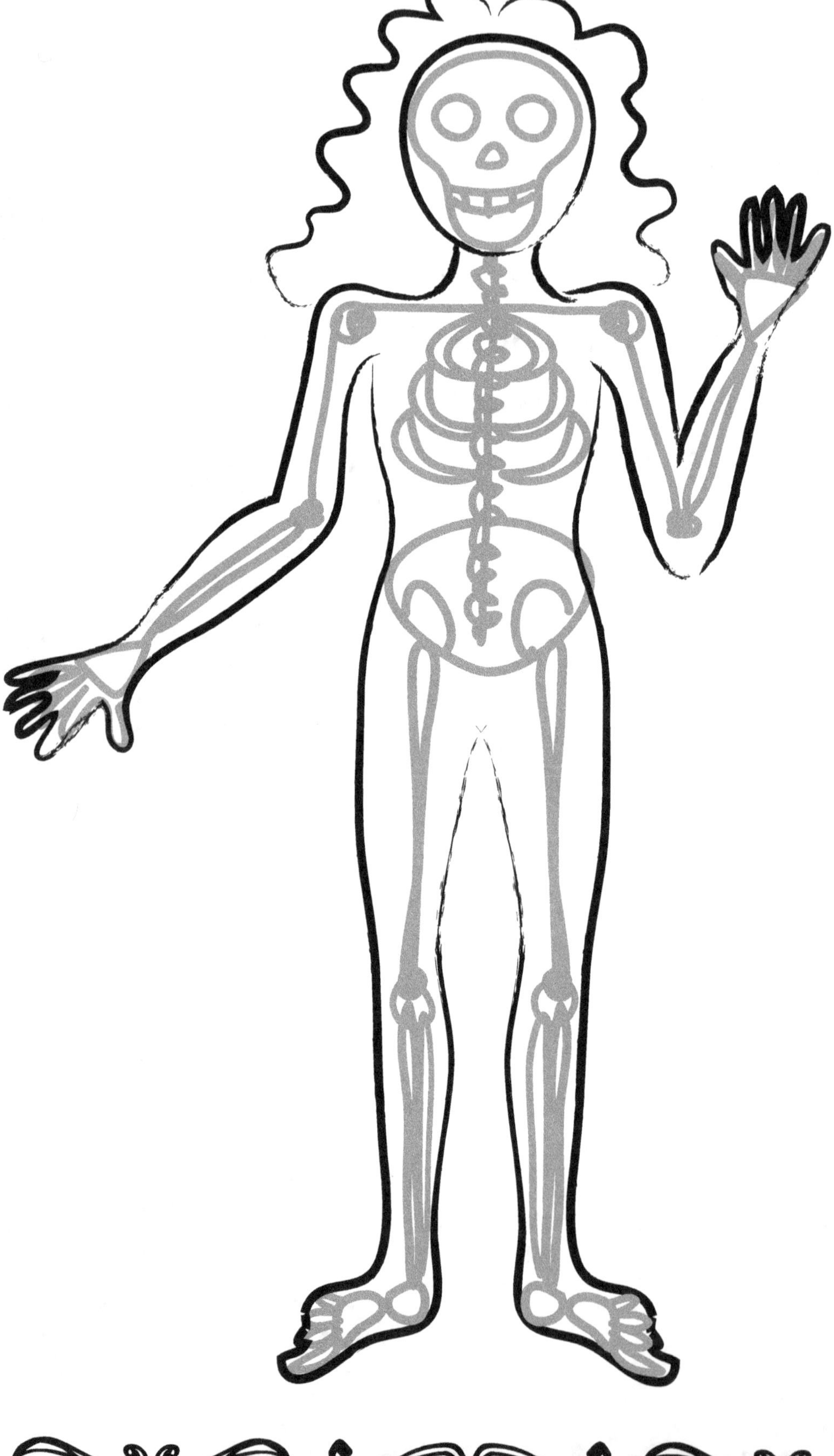

Practice drawing the body and hair
on top of the skeleton:

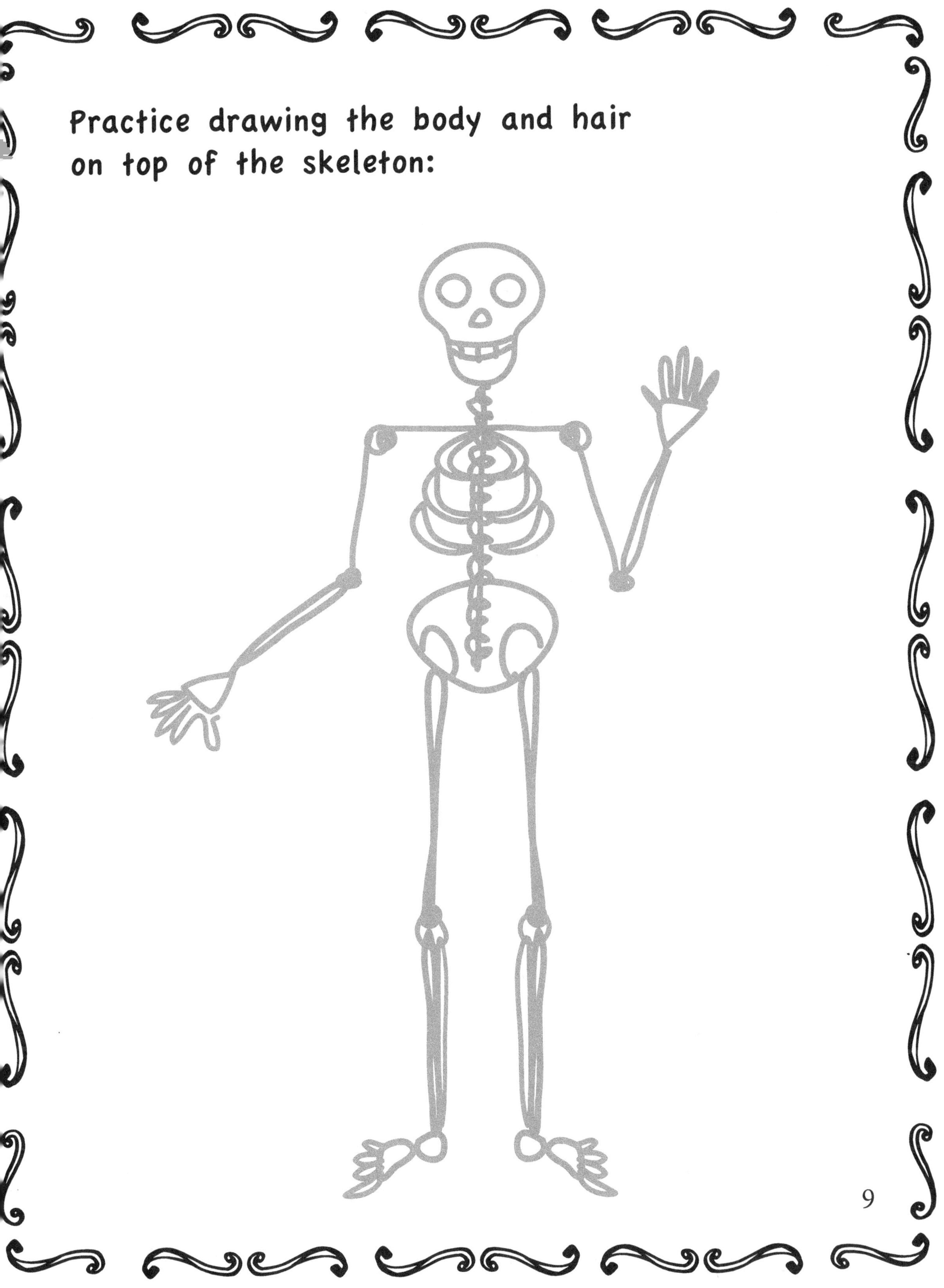

To help us draw at first, rather than drawing an entire
skeleton, we will use a stick figure as the base, or the
frame of our person. Once you jot down the stick figure,
you can add the body (muscle/skin/hair) on top of the
stick figure. Once we are done with learning to draw the
person's shape, we can add clothing to complete the drawing.
Use a pencil, so that you can erase all of the extra
lines when you are done.

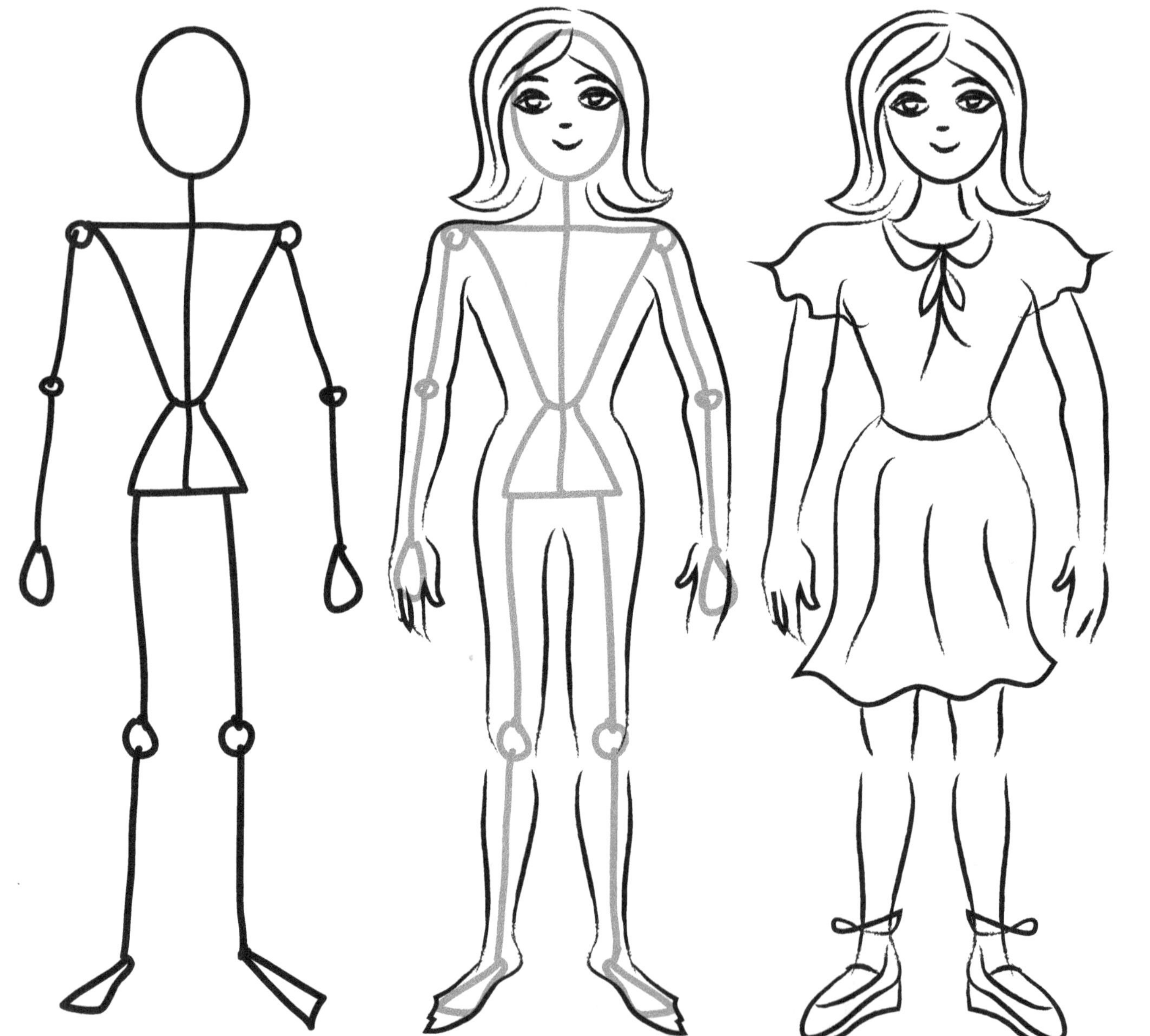

For the most part, people are symmetrical - what
you draw on one side of the body, you can repeat
on the other side.

Practice page

Go ahead and add the
two more steps to complete
the person.

How to draw people in action. Drawing from what you
see is the best way to learn. Once you get the basic
anatomy, you can then draw people from your imagination.
Try this. Put on an online video of any sports activity.
Start with a slow activity like yoga. You can pause the
video at any point to get a better view. Try to draw the
action first as stick figures, to get the basic gesture of the
poses. Don't get hung up on the details yet. Once you get the
gestures, you can start to add more details of the body
anatomy, clothing, and lightly indicate faces and hair.
After you get some practice, this process will happen
seamlessly, without the "stick figure."

Practice Activity.
Put on your favorite online video sports or yoga channel.
Now draw the person exercising.
Pause any time you need to get a better look
at the pose. Try to get a quick gesture of the
pose first. Then you can get into more details of the
body and the clothing, face and hair. Use a pencil
so you can erase the stick figure after you are done.

Name of pose:

____

Seated pose

Practice drawing the seated pose:

Body in action.
Walking pose.

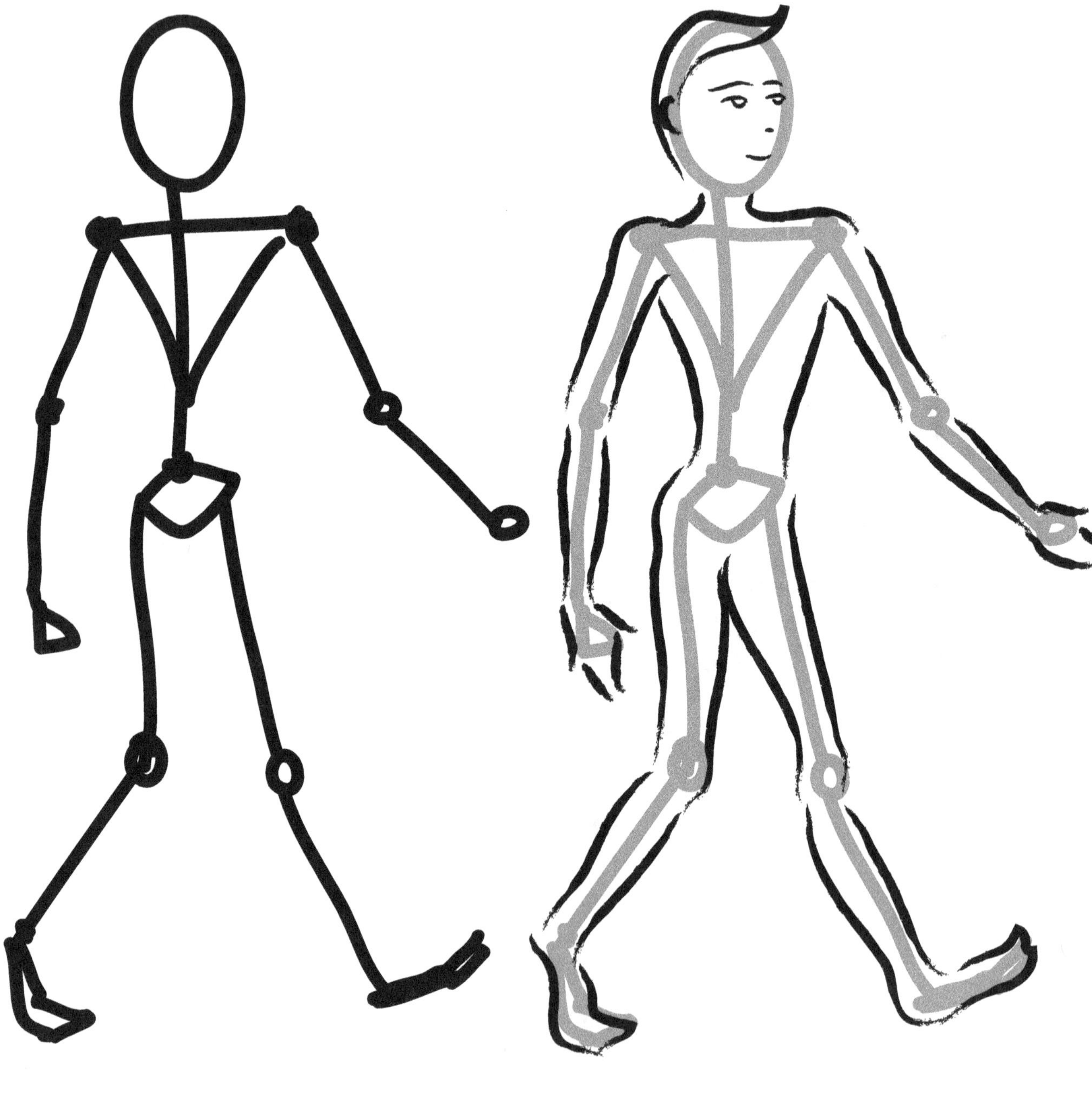

Practice drawing the walking pose:

Body in action.
Running pose.

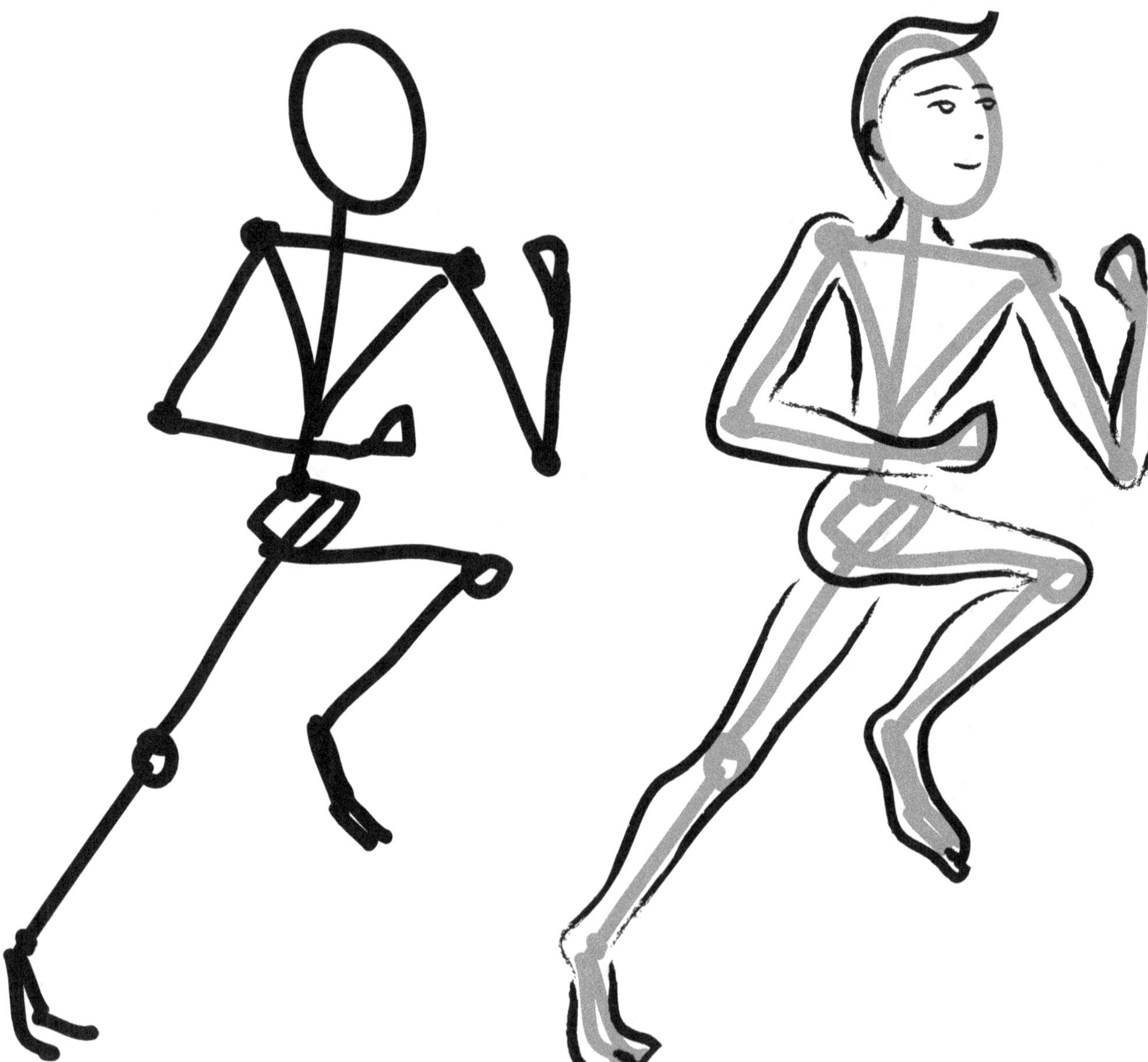

Practice drawing the running pose:

HEAD & FACE

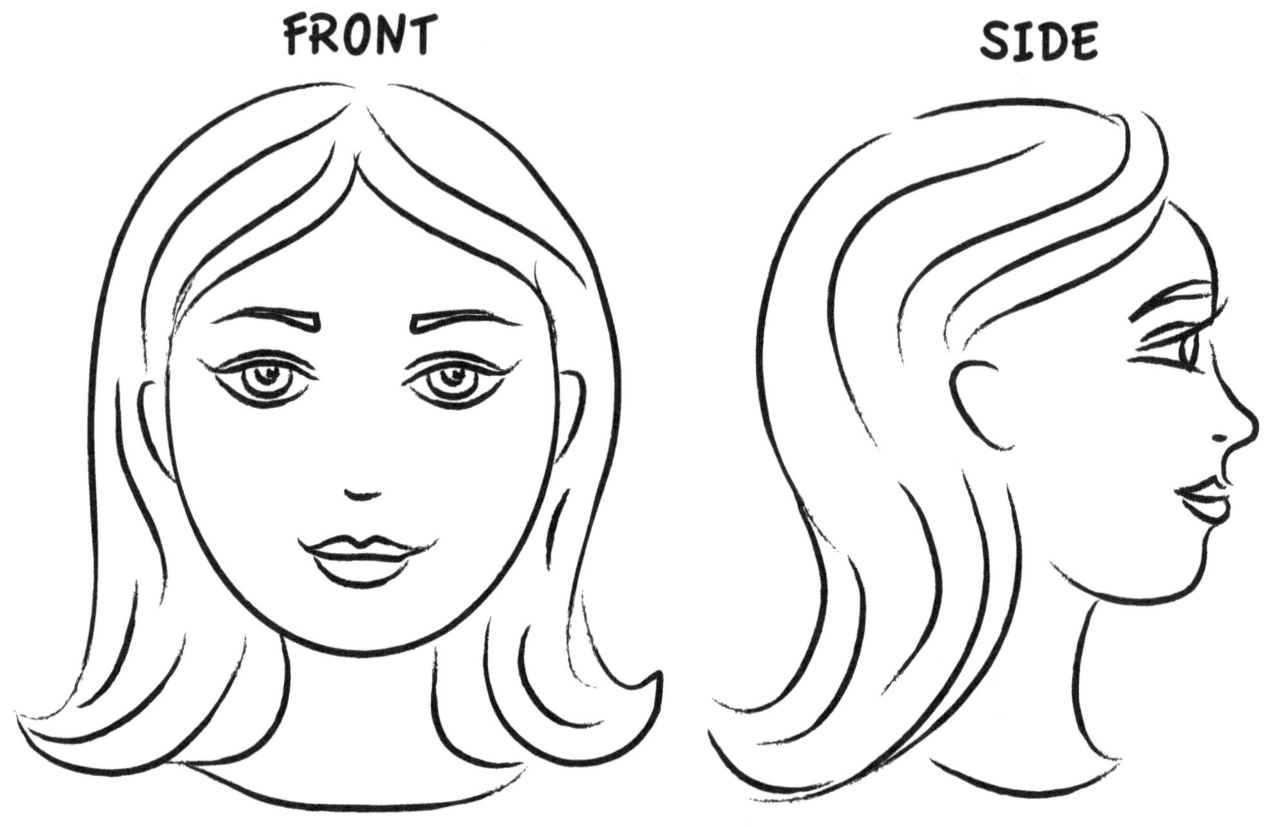

There is no one right way to draw a person. However, there are some basic anatomical rules. Head is not flat, it is a spherical shape, the eyes are not on top of the head, they are across the middle. When you draw, you have to account for the 3D shape of the head. Hair doesn't just grow at the top, it grows around the head and on its sides. The eyes are about one eye distance apart from each other. There are many ways you can indicate a nose, even a small line is enough. Tops of the ears line up with the corners of the eyes.

Face drawing practice

FRONT

Draw in the face on the head. Try to place the features in their proper locations by referring to the previous page.

SIDE

Now draw the profile view of the face. You can look at the previous page for reference.

VIEWS

You can draw multiple facial views.
Front view, 3/4 view, side view.
You can draw a person looking up
or down. You can even have them
turn around and only see the back.

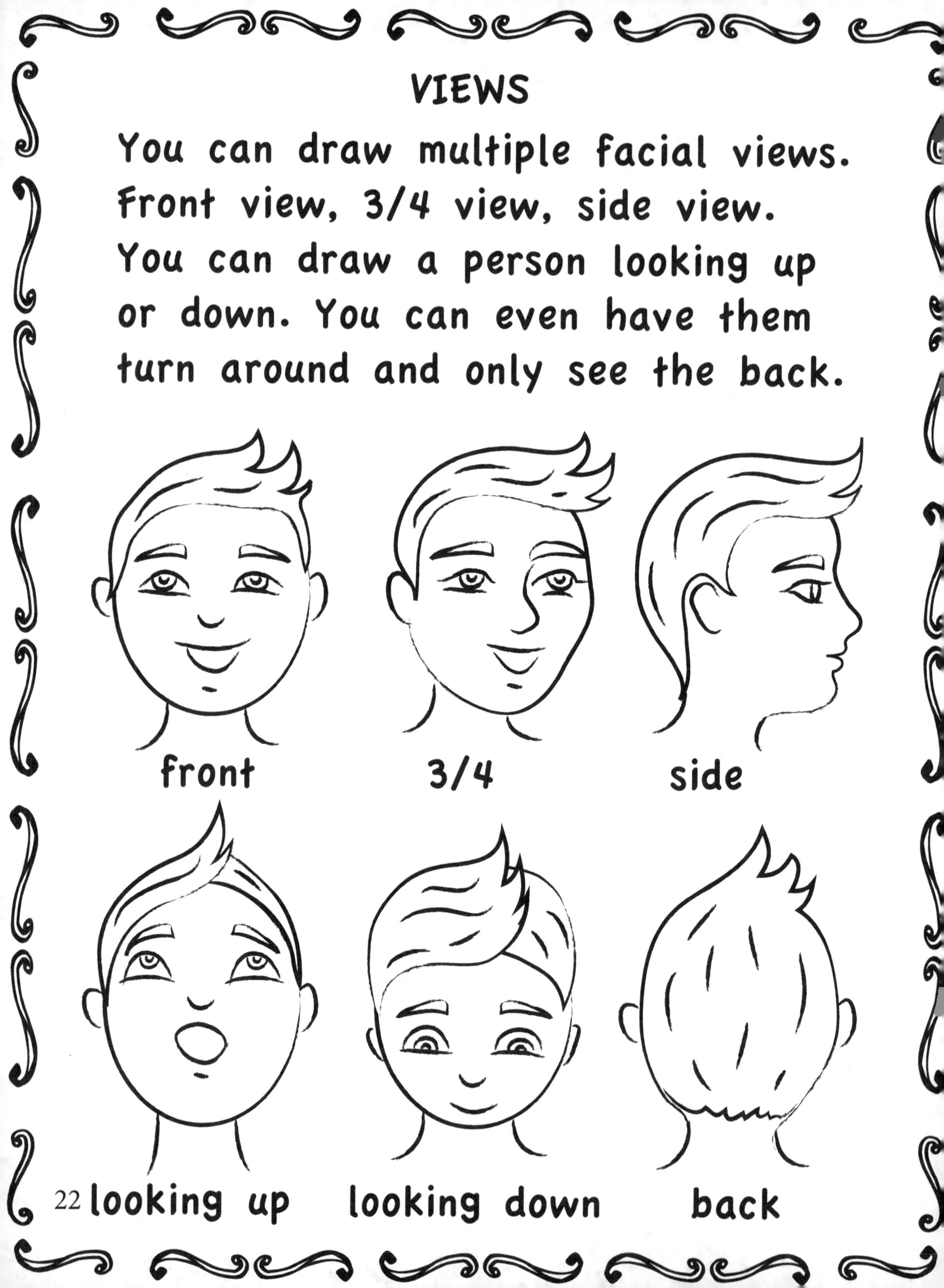

Practice page.

Try to draw different views here.
Complete the pictures by adding
facial features and hair.

front   3/4   side

looking up   looking down   back

Right and wrong way to draw hair.

The way you draw hair can make or break a drawing of your person. Hair drawing doesn't have to be complex, however, if you do decide to get into detail, do it the right way. Hair has to be drawn in the direction in which it grows, this is especially important for straight and wavy hair. For curly or extremely curly hair, you can play around with textures, by making different sized swirls. But never just randomly draw in the hair in haphazard direction. Draw hair by strands, as if you are combing it yourself as you draw it. It will make for quite a pleasing and artistic picture too! You can also indicate a hair shape by making a simple outline, without even getting into detail. Assuming the rest of your drawing is simple as well.

Right and wrong way to draw hair.

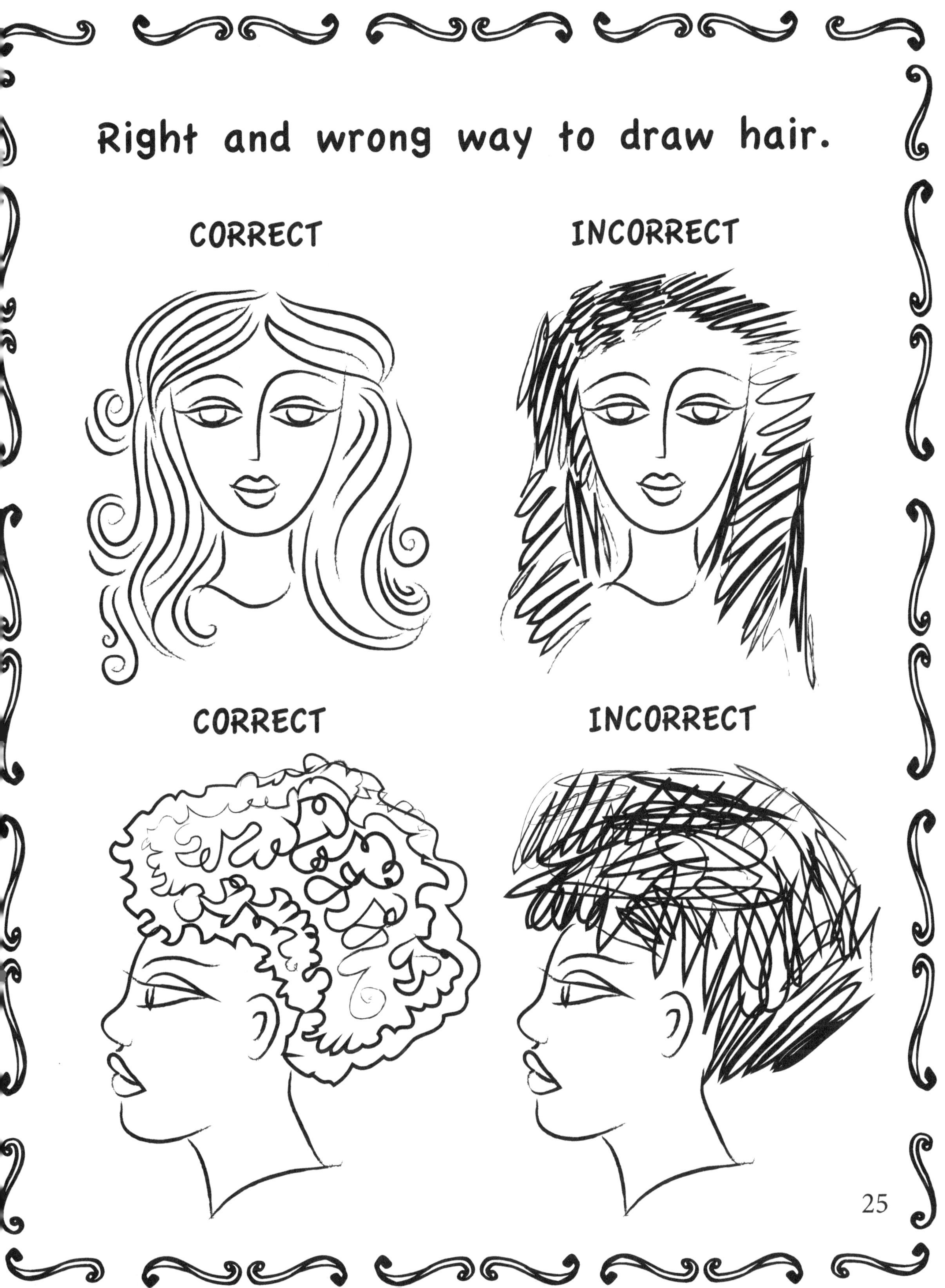

Play with hair styles and textures.

Practice page for hair styles.
Add unique textures and different
shaped lines to show hair styles.

Once you get the basic rules, you can play around. The best way to do it is to exaggerate facial features to make unique and funny faces. That's what makes your people interesting and stylized.

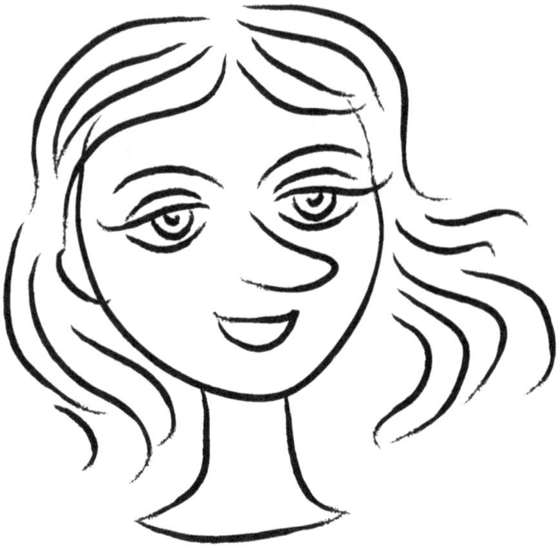

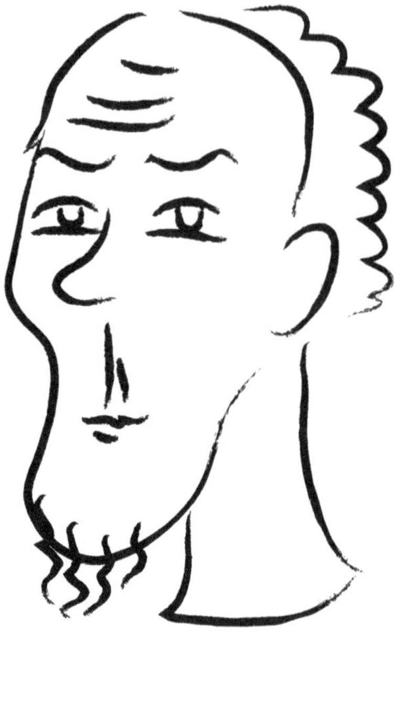

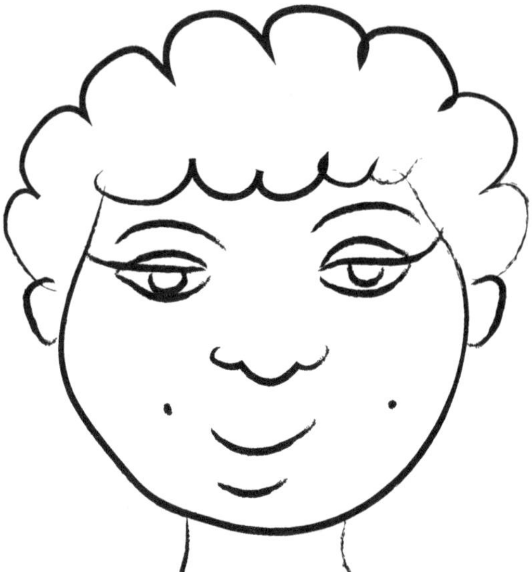

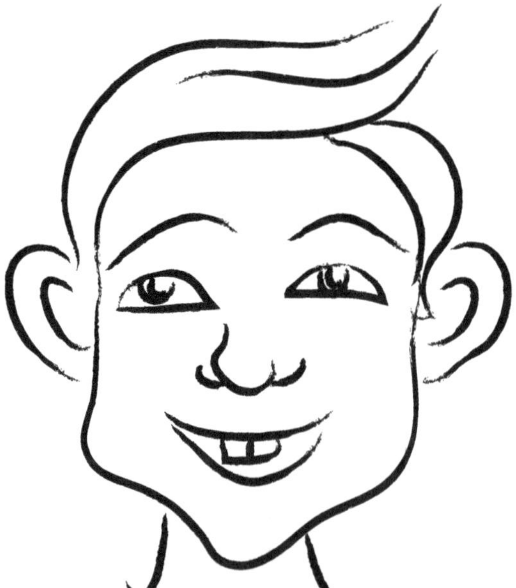

Practice drawing exaggerated facial features.
Don't forget to add all the musts: eyes,
eyebrows, ears, nose, lips and hair!

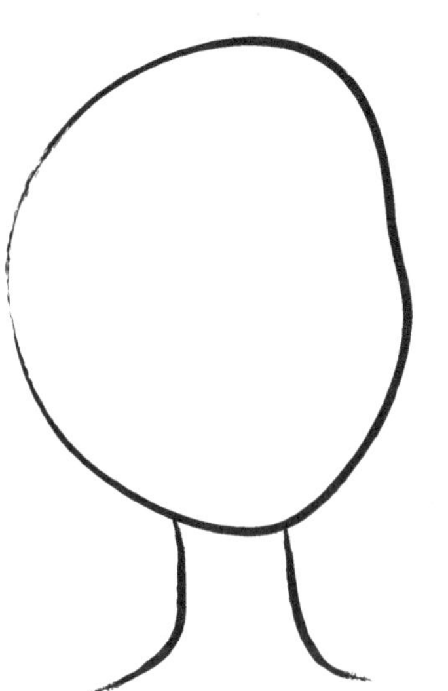

Draw a face
with a big nose.

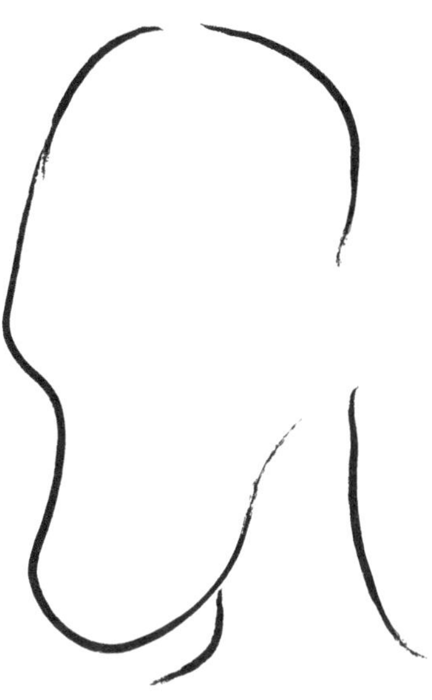

Draw an old
wrinkled face.

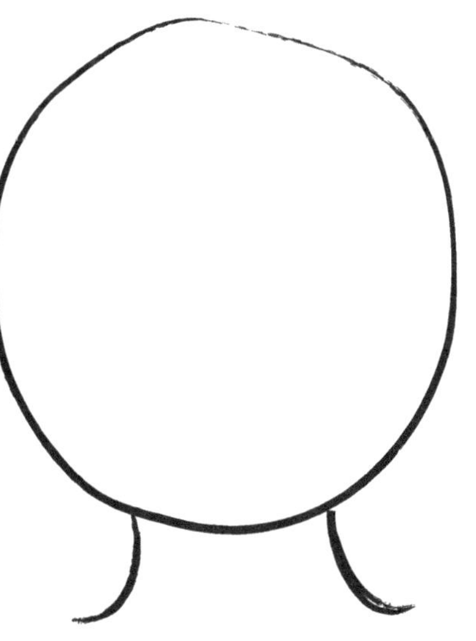

Draw a face
with curly hair
and dimples.

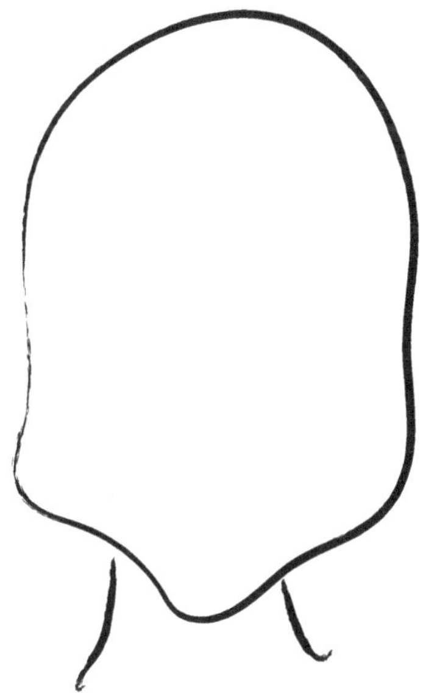

Draw a face
with big ears
and a goofy smile.

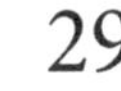

Drawing eyes

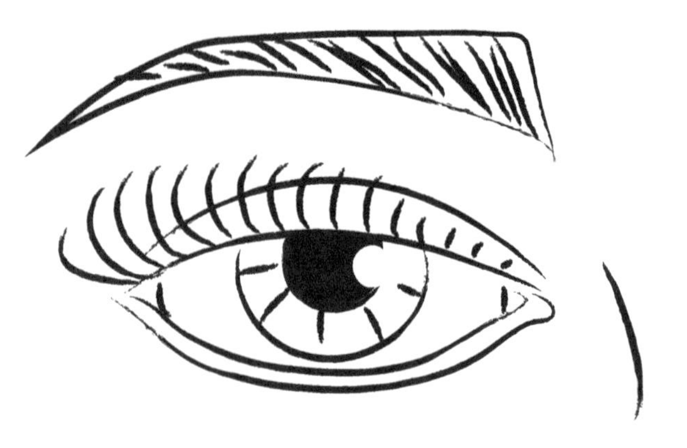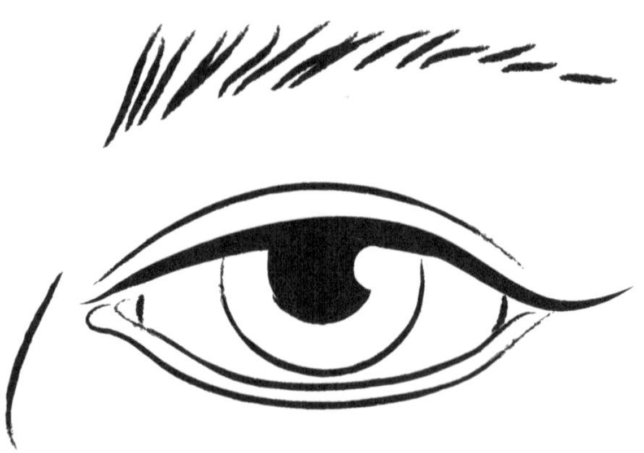

Eye balls are called that for a reason, they are spherical
shapes which are located inside the eye sockets.
Picture the depth and roundness of the eye as you draw it.
Picture the eye ball sitting inside the eye, covered by
eyelids, and then eyelashes. The eye ball consists of a pupil,
iris, and sclera (the white part of the eye). It is a good idea
to place a highlight in the same direction on both eyes, right
at the top of the pupil, to indicate light and emphasize the shape.
Do so either by leaving the circular small shapes white
or by erasing the small shapes in the iris and lightly drawing
an outline around the white areas.
You never see the entire iris/pupil, there is usually some eyelid
overlap at the top or even bottom, unless you are drawing an
extreme emotion, in which case you can break this rule.
When drawing eyebrows, you can do it in a few ways. Either draw
the outline first, then add the hair in its growth direction,
or you can simply draw the hair without the outline or even
just indicate the eyebrows with a simple line.
The eyelashes can be indicated in two ways. You can draw one line,
at the lid line, by just making it thicker, as if you are drawing an
eye liner on your eyelid. You can also draw the eyelashes individually,
by curling them in the outward direction. Lashes gradually get longer
toward the outer corner of the eye.

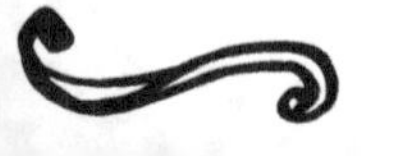

Eye drawing practice

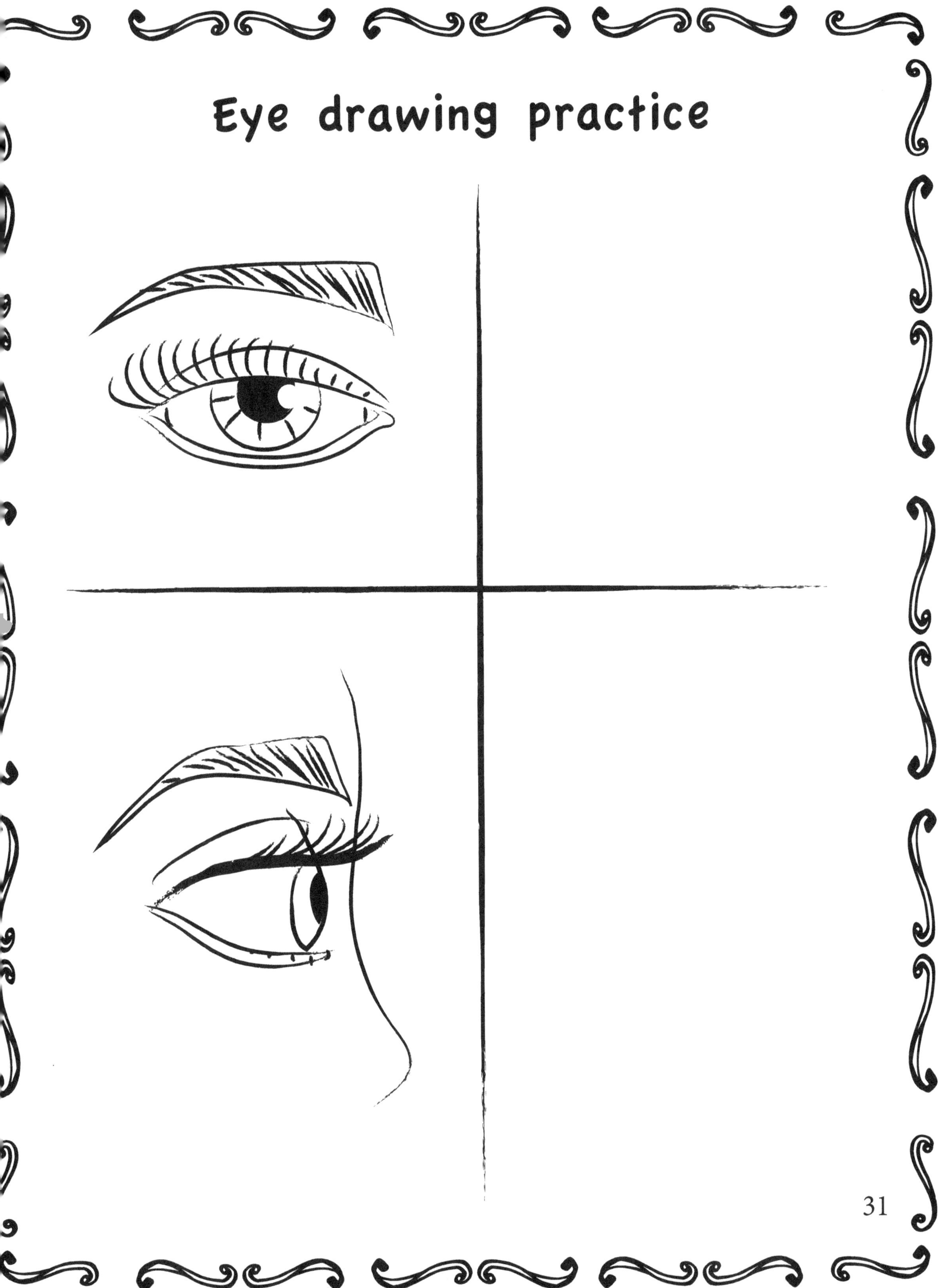

Drawing noses

There are so many different ways to draw noses.
Noses are fun to draw and they give such character
to your people drawings. Noses are entirely optional,
depending on the types of drawings you are doing.
If it is a quick sketch, you can omit the nose altogether.
A nose can be shown by just a simple line too, without
going into detail - it can still be expressed.
Noses can be exaggerated if you are drawing cartoons
or caricatures - to show the character of the person.

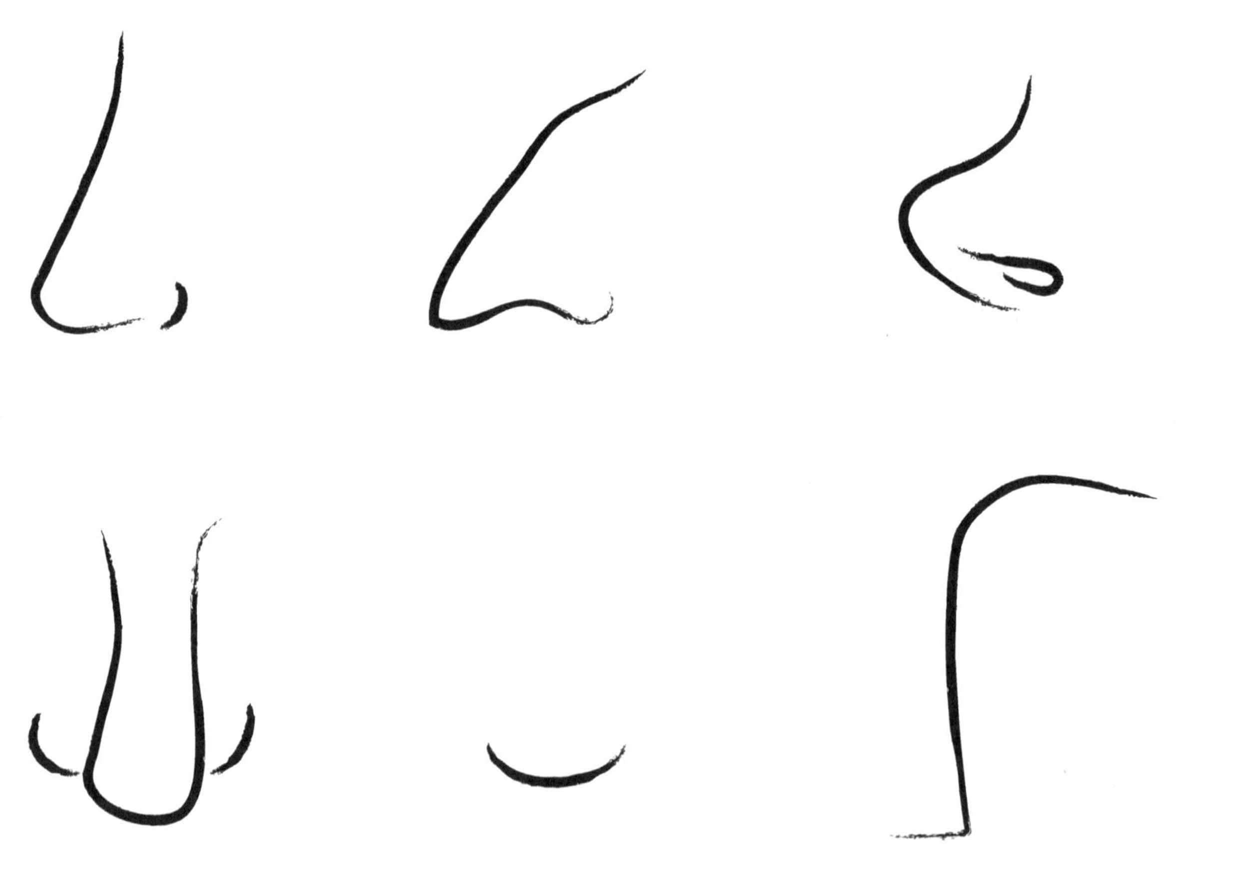

Nose drawing practice

Turn on any online video and pay attention to people's noses. If you see an interesting nose, pause the video and draw it, along with the face. Try to use the least amount of lines to express the character of the nose. Challenge yourself to draw a variety of different nose shapes.

Long nose

Big and wide nose

Perky small nose

Nose with a bump

Drawing lips

Like noses, lips come in many different shapes.
Lips can express emotions, so we have to pay
attention to them, especially when drawing portraits.
Show a smile by putting small lines at the corners
of the mouth.

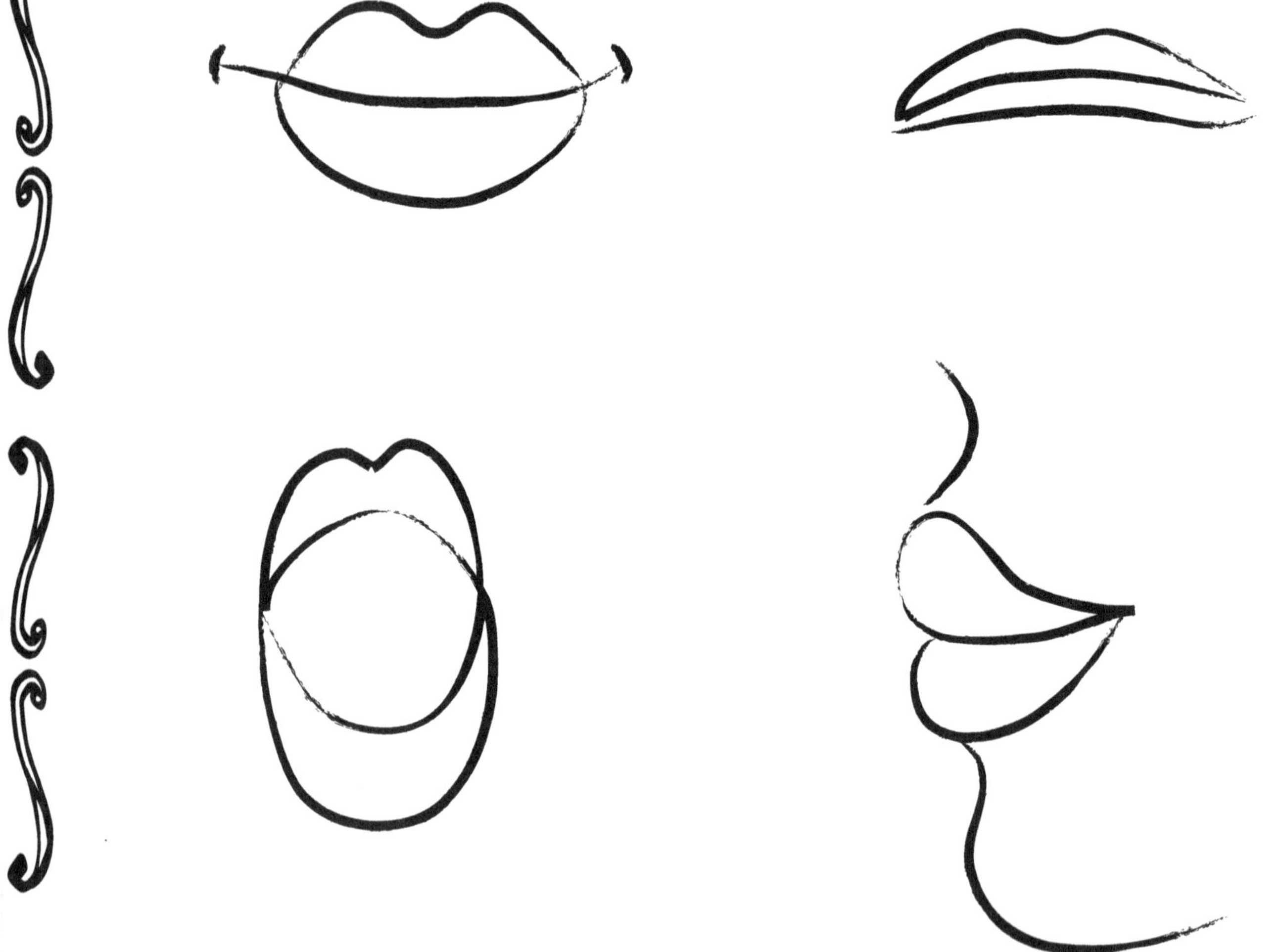

Lip drawing practice

Go online and see what kind of lips/mouths people have and how they express themselves there. Draw the various expressions you see, for example:

Smiling lips

Sad lips

Surprised lips

Side view of lips

Drawing ears

Ears are not always the first things we notice,
however they are an important part of the anatomy.
They can also be expressive, though you don't
always have to draw them.
When you do draw them, a couple of simple lines
are often enough to indicate their existence.
Unless covered by hair, it's a good idea to show
at least some of the ears.
Often, a simple line will do.

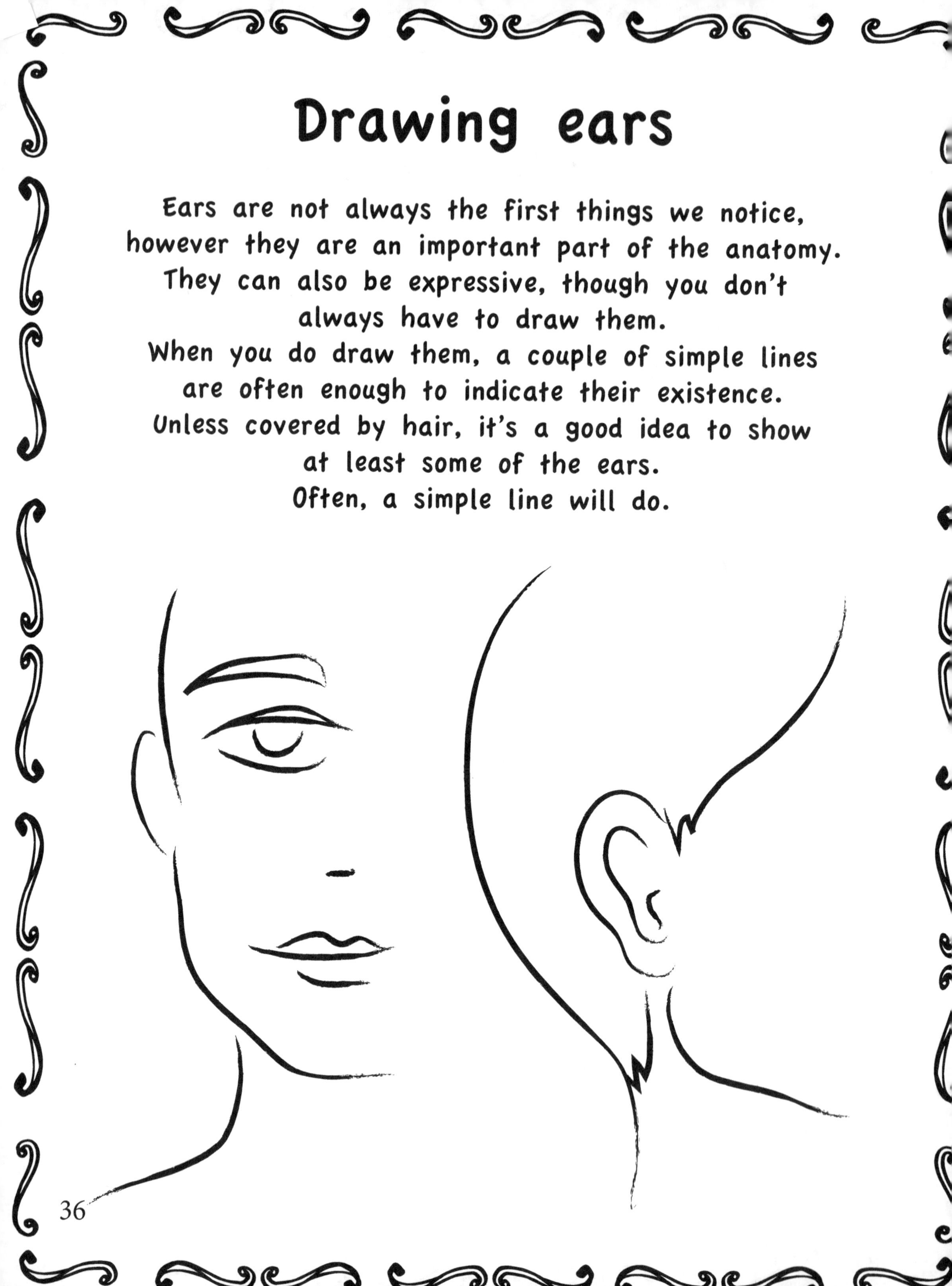

Ear drawing practice

Take a mirror and look at your own ears.
How do they look? Do they pop out or
are more flush to the head?
Draw your ears or photos of ears
you found on the Internet.

Ear side view   Ear front view

What's in a hand?

The thumb is the general of the
hand, he functions more independently and
has a wider range of motion from
the rest of the fingers. But all of the fingers
function in unison with each other.
Men have larger hands than women, with
thicker fingers and wider wrists.
Lightly indicate finger nails by simple lines.

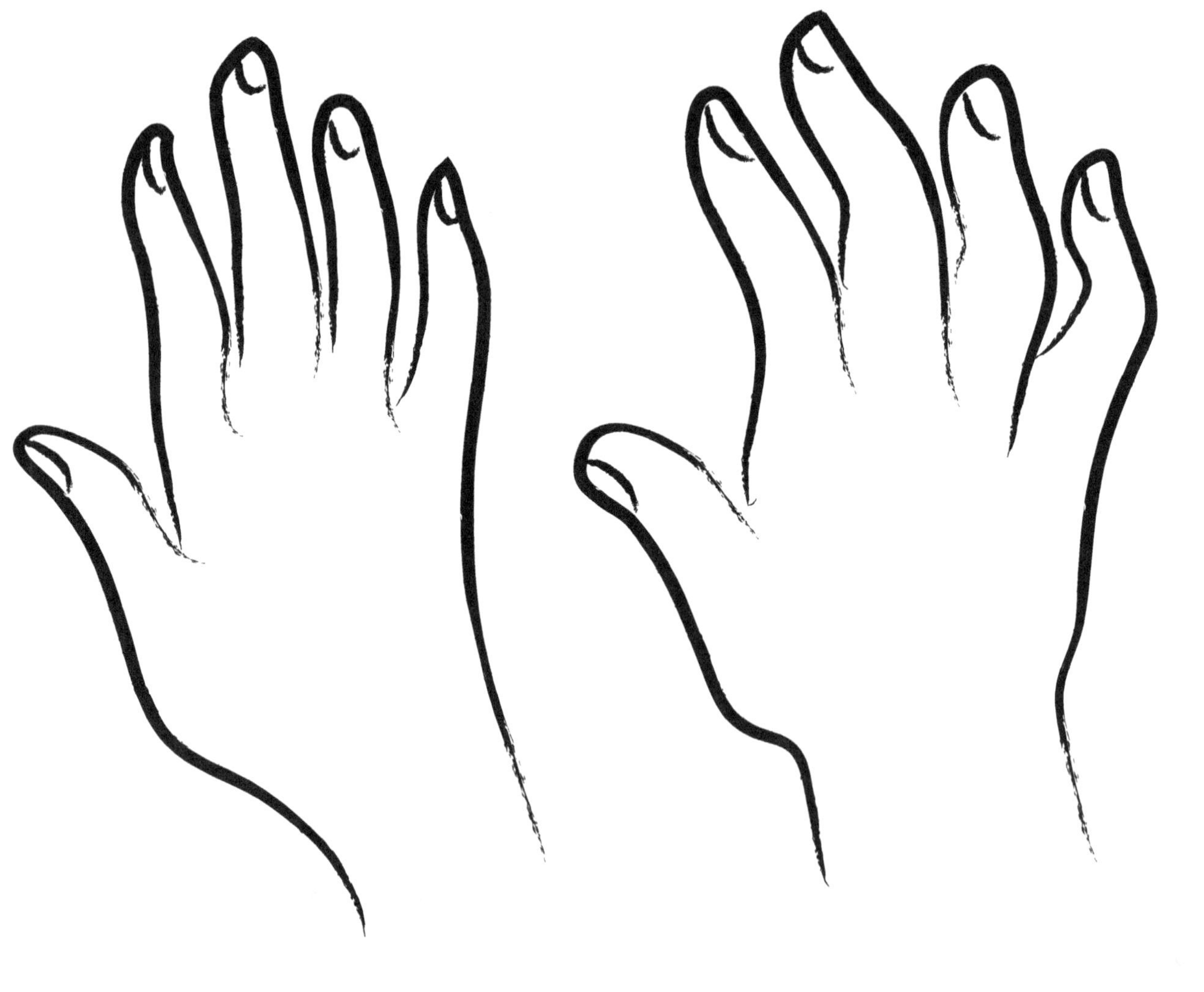

Draw your hand

Now it's time for you to draw your hand.
Draw it in a simple relaxed position.
Pay attention to the relative length
of the fingers and their
relationship to one another.
Don't get discouraged if you don't get it
the first time around.
Use extra paper to practice more and more
until you start to see progress.

Let's draw hands!

People are simply terrified of drawing hands!
But it doesn't have to be scary.
The best thing you can do to learn to draw
hands is to draw hands as much as possible.
You are lucky, you can look at your own
hands and draw them any time!

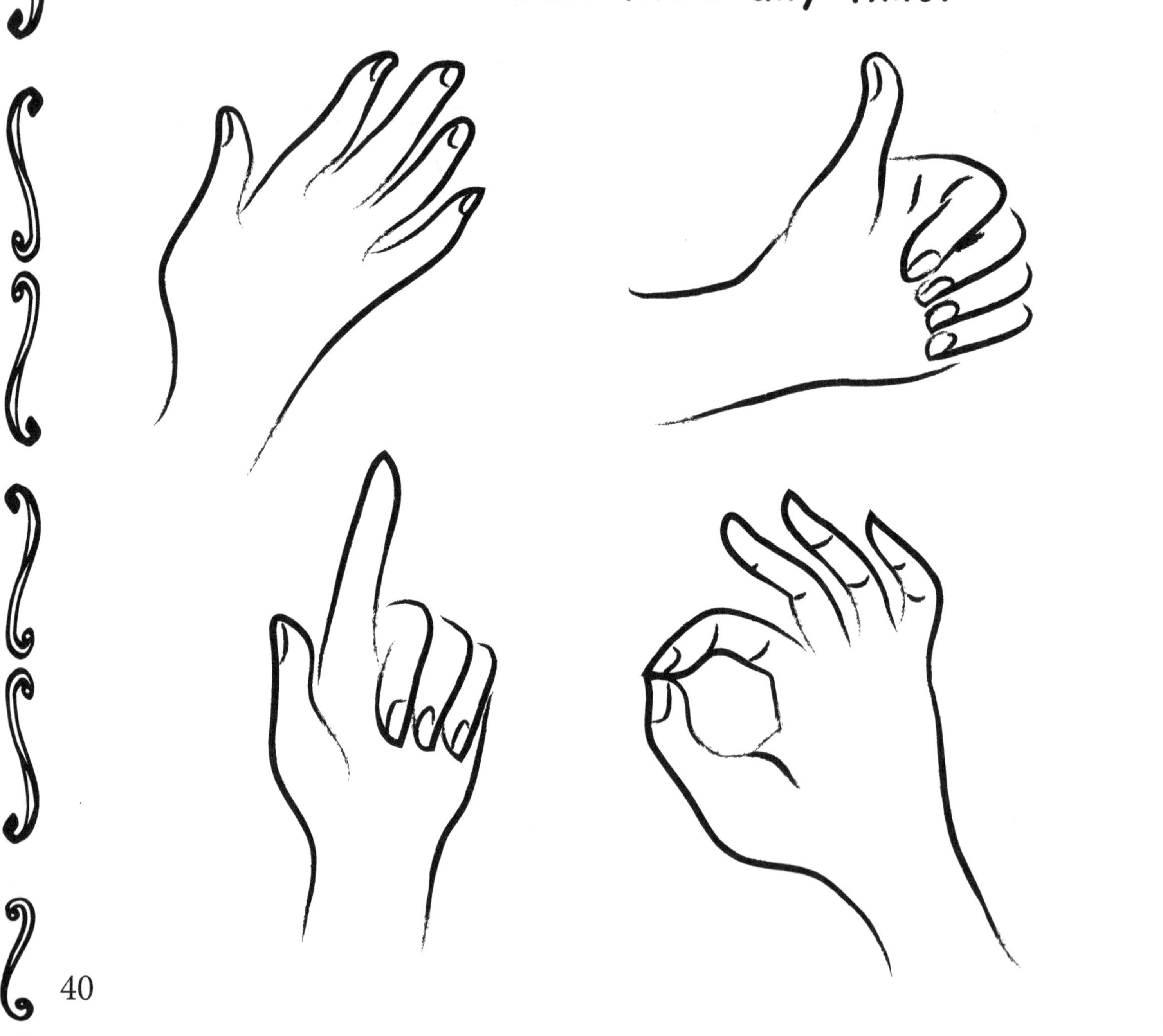

Hand drawing practice

Now make different gestures with your hands, and draw each one. If you are right handed, draw your left hand, and vise versa. Try cupping your hand, pointing your finger, giving a thumbs up, you get the idea! Before you know it, you will get a great handle on drawing hands!

1.

2.

3.

4.

Let's draw feet!

You're in luck, since you have models at your disposal! Take off your shoes and socks and draw your own feet. Test out different poses, flexed, pointed, side view, front view, etc.

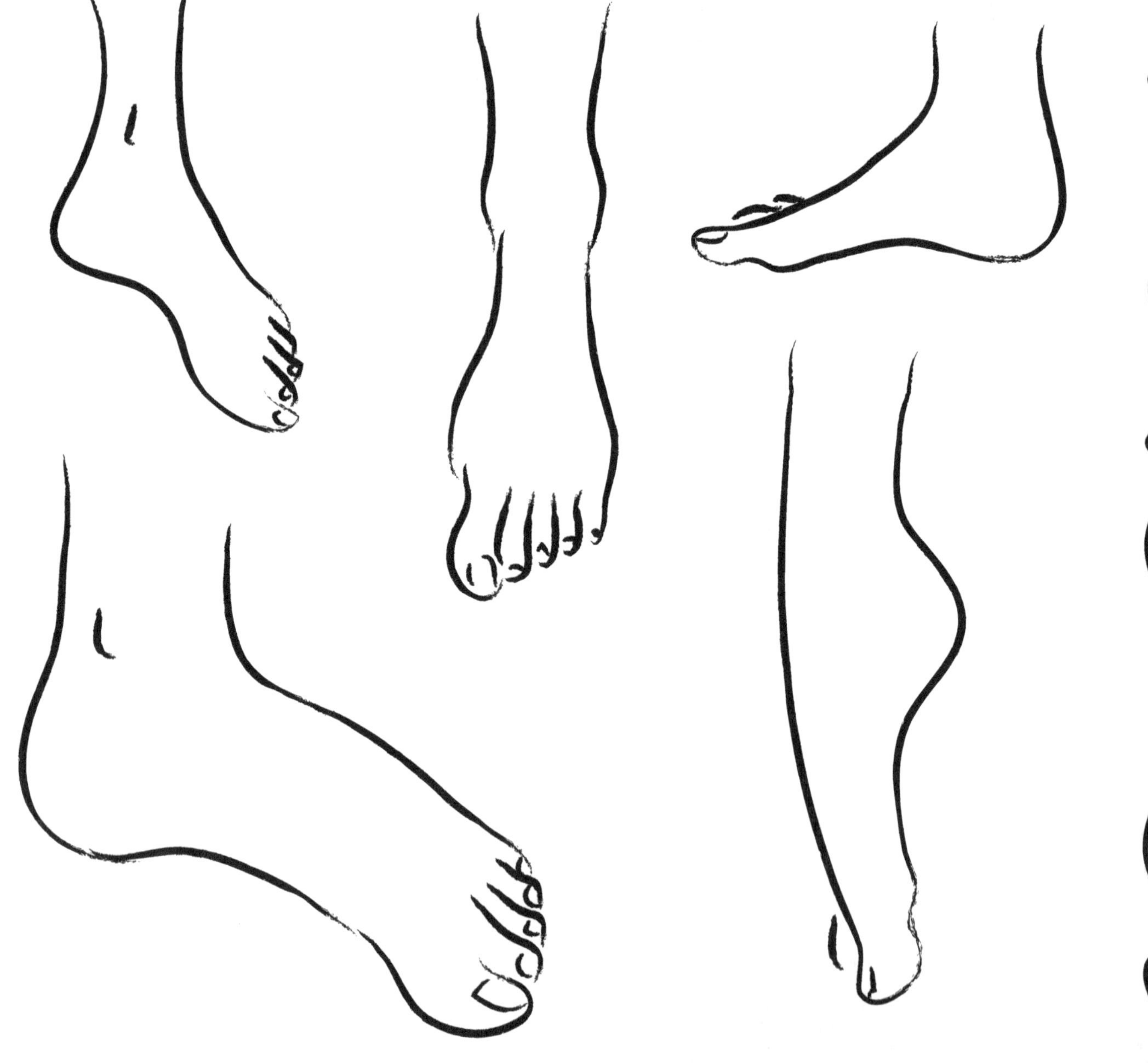

Foot drawing practice

Now let's get drawing! Look at your feet and draw them at different angles. Remember that toes are different lengths, starting with largest and getting smaller and smaller. The foot gently slopes, there are no sharp angles. Have fun!!

Left foot   Right foot

Kids vs. Adults

Drawing a kid's face and an adult's face is a little bit different. Kids' faces have other proportions to those of adults.

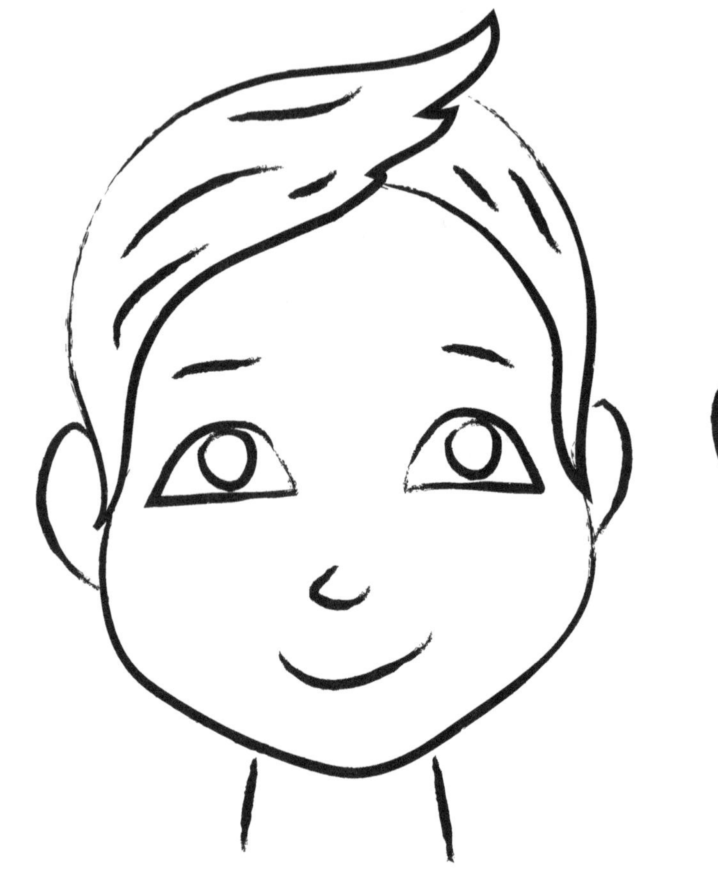

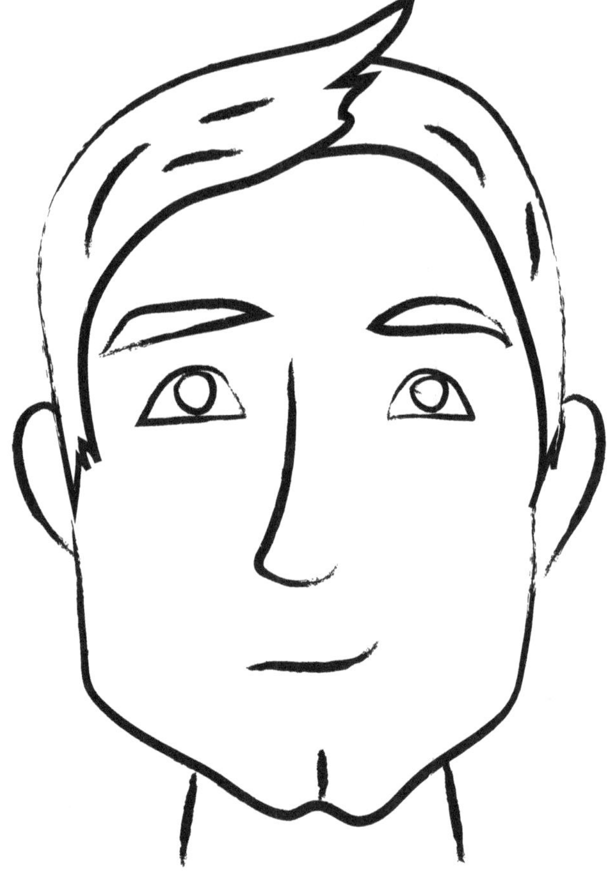

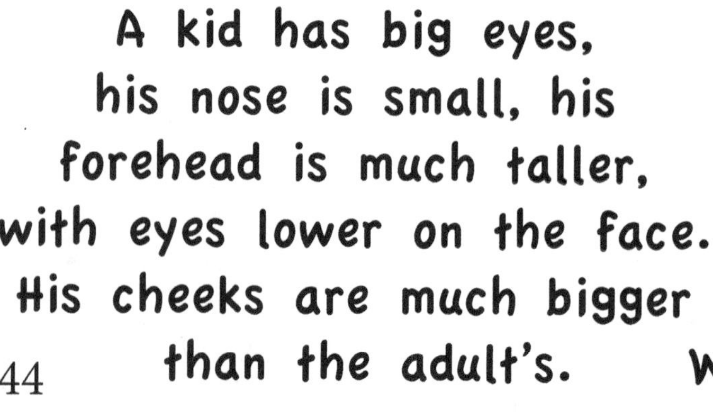

A kid has big eyes, his nose is small, his forehead is much taller, with eyes lower on the face. His cheeks are much bigger than the adult's.

Adults have smaller eyes which appear higher on the face, bushier eyebrows, bigger noses, smaller cheeks and ears. Wider neck and a stronger chin.

Practice drawing kid and adult features.

Drawing clothing

Although this book is about drawing people, not drawing clothing, people do wear clothing, don't they? So let's dedicate a couple of pages to drawing clothing. Like skin and muscle, clothing drapes the body, it doesn't lie flat, it goes around the body. So, by using a few simple lines, we can show that a person is indeed wearing clothing.

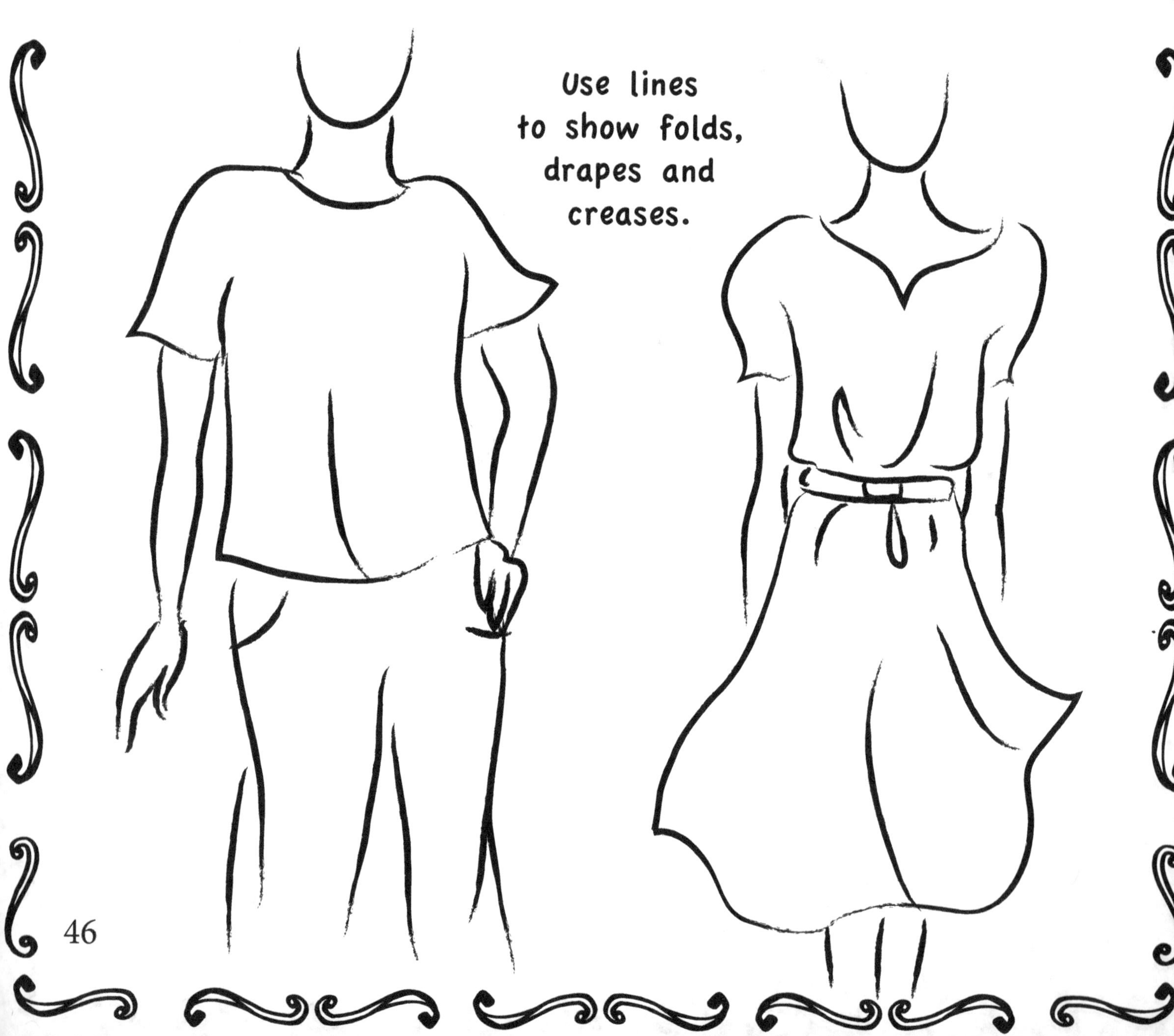

Drawing clothing practice

For this practice, find a piece of clothing in the closet, such as a shirt, skirt, pants or a tee. Draw it flat, then draw it after a person has put it on their body. Does it look different? Do you notice any lines that appear with movement?

Drawing people from the back

Since we draw people from the back less
often than we do from the front,
sometimes it can be a challenge.
Here are some examples of back views
which you can then practice drawing yourself.

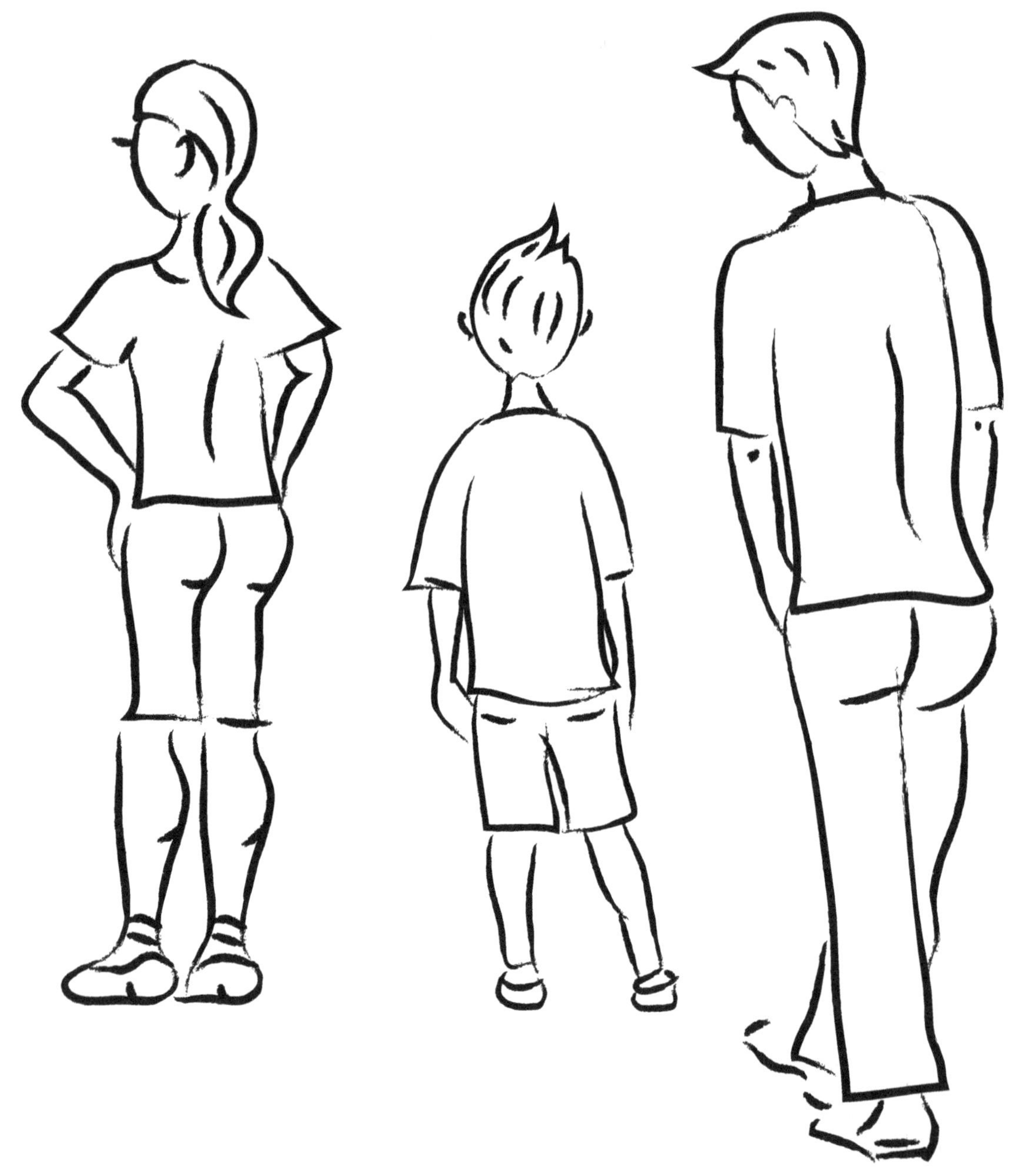

Drawing practice

Now find some videos of people walking around
online and draw them specifically from the back.
It's good to know how to draw people from
all angles! Use a lot of paper to practice on.

Be aware of body positions

When we go to do life drawings, we go there to practice, to draw people in any positions in which they are posing.

But when we make illustrations or portraits, we should be aware of the way our drawings will be interpreted by the viewer.

For example, let's look at the view from the back with bent arms:

AVOID THIS   DRAW THIS

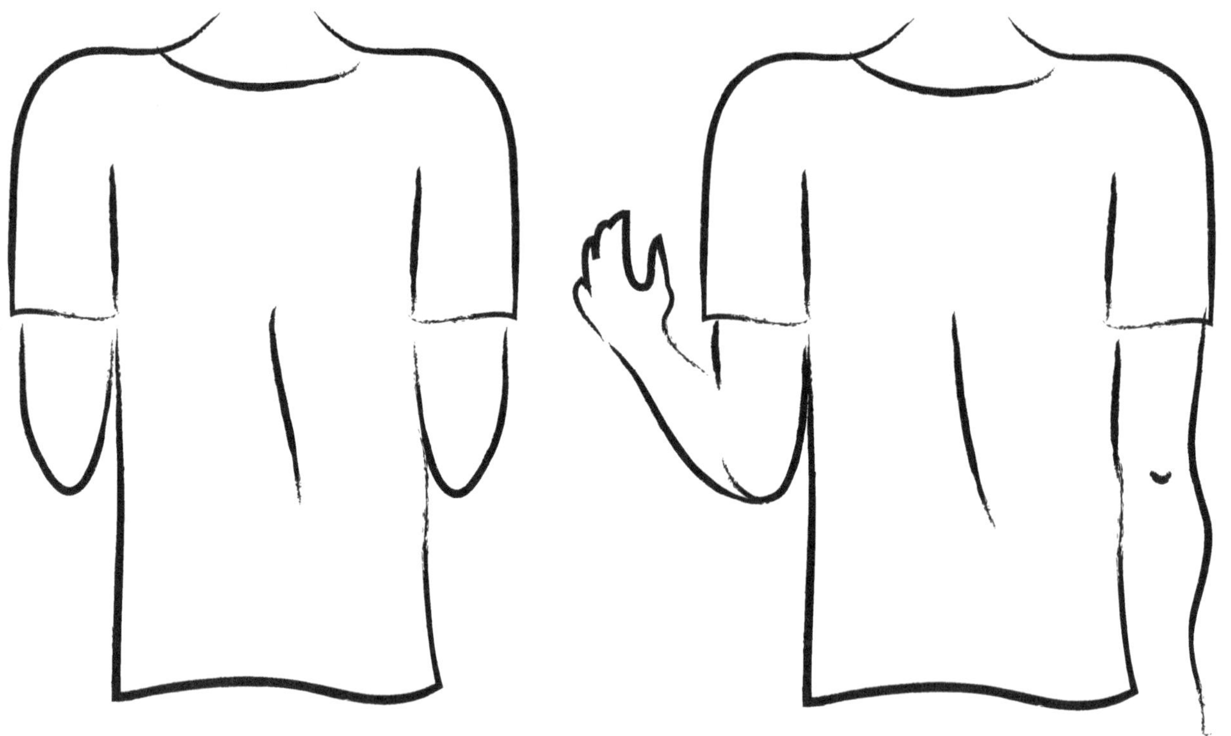

It's best to show the bend in a 3/4 view, so you can at least see some of the rest of the arm or arms.

Foreshortening

This one is also tricky, and should only be used when you intend to show a special pose, and should only be done correctly. It is when you see a close up of a hand or a foot and the body is drawn in perspective.

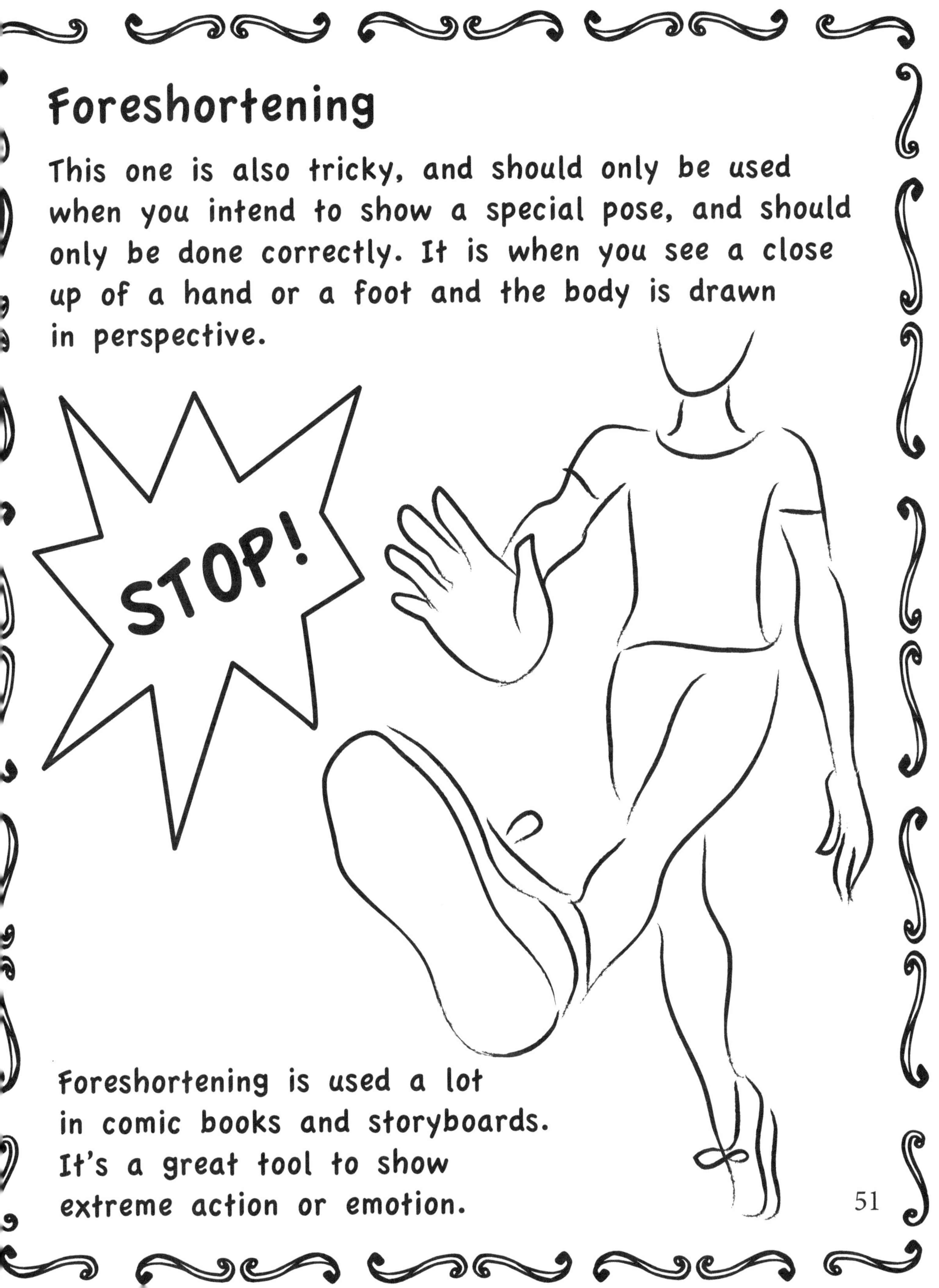

Foreshortening is used a lot in comic books and storyboards. It's a great tool to show extreme action or emotion.

How to get a likeness of a person?

So, once you can draw people, how do you draw them to look like themselves? If a friend asks you to draw their portrait, how do you make sure to do a good job of getting the likeness?

Practice, practice, practice. In addition, there a few rules that will help you with getting their likeness.

Tip 1. Find something unique about their face and make sure to emphasize it. How? Exaggerate it a little. Keeping in mind that the drawing still has to be flattering. But to get a likeness of them, the feature has to be even more visible than it is in real life.

Like in this drawing of a famous singer...
Her unique nose, eyes and lips are emphasized.

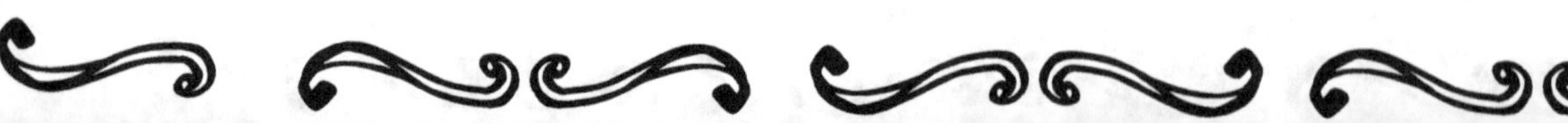

How to get a likeness of a person?

Tip 2. Proportions. Always pay attention to the proportions of the face. Every person has his or her unique spacing between the eyes, nose, width of the forehead, etc. The distance between the features is just as important as the features themselves in getting the likeness of the person.

Tip 3. Have fun! Add some characteristic accessories, clothes, funny hairstyles, to show the character of the person you are drawing. Even if their likeness is not spot on, the personality will come through with the helpful other items you add to the picture. Do they like to draw? Have them holding a pencil. Or if they are into video games, give them a controller. You get the picture! Draw a lot and enjoy the process! You can video chat with friends and have them pose for you at the same time!

Let's celebrate our differences!

We are all beautiful and unique, we have different skin colors, different features, sizes, shapes, ages, hair textures, clothes, styles, smiles, noses, lips, teeth and ears. We come from different ethnic backgrounds, countries and continents. We have differet tastes and traditions, abilities and conditions. The more you draw a wide variety of people, the better you will become at getting the different personalities to come through in your work. While not disparaging styles like Anime, or kids books which for some reason try to make everyone look the same, we should strive to draw people as they are, not as fake robots or dolls. So find some videos of a variety of different people and draw them as much as possible.

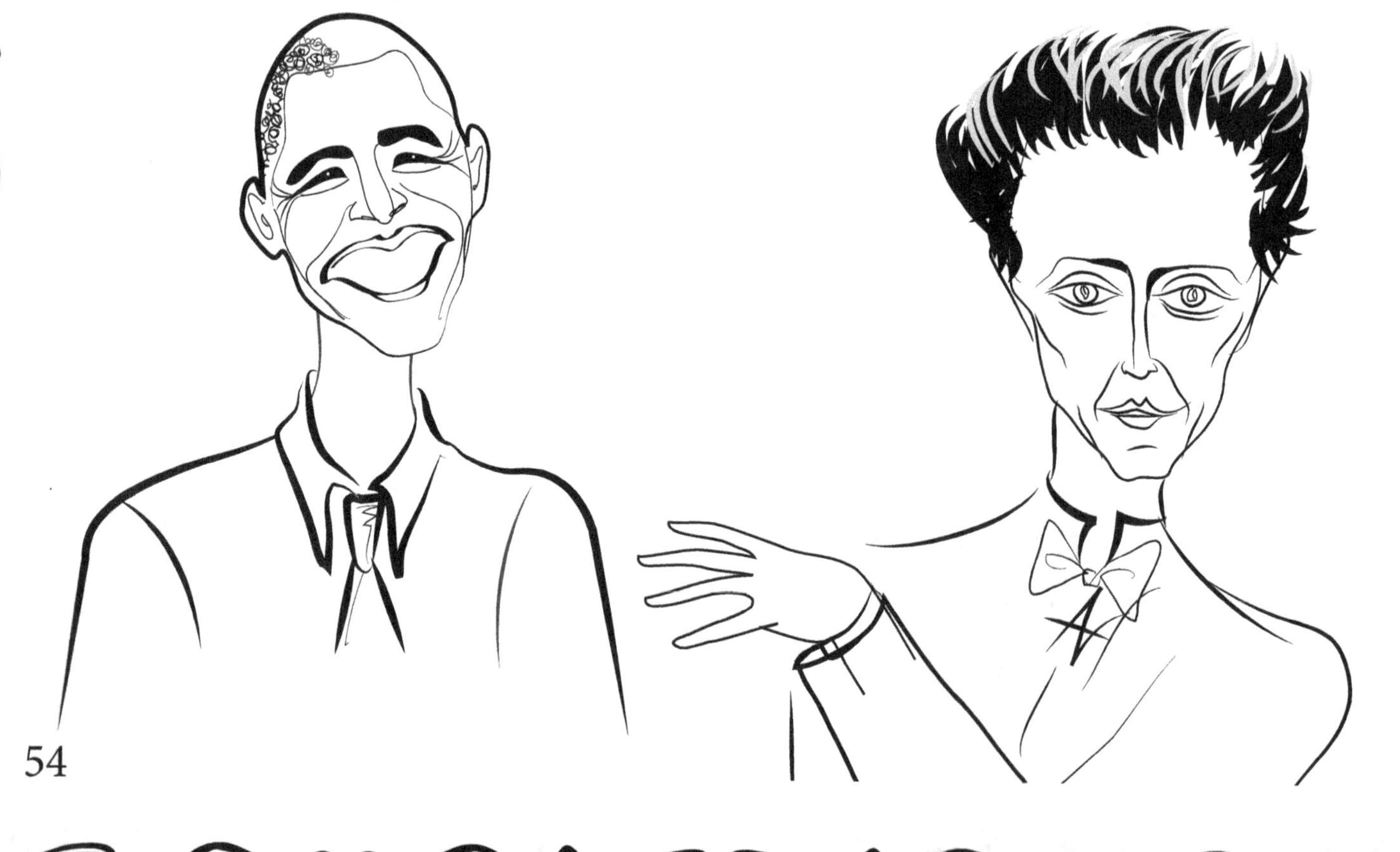

Portrait Practice

Arrange a video call with a friend or a family member. Prepare some pencils, eraser, pen or markers.
While you chat, try to get their personality and sketch out some portraits. If you feel like you're not on the right track, and you are too far into it to erase, you can stop that drawing and start a new one. But try to do your best to draw without stopping the video.
It's always better to draw from a live person.
You can also practice from photos of course, but for this exercise, use a live drawing session. You will be surprised how, after a while, you will get quite good at catching the person's essence on paper!

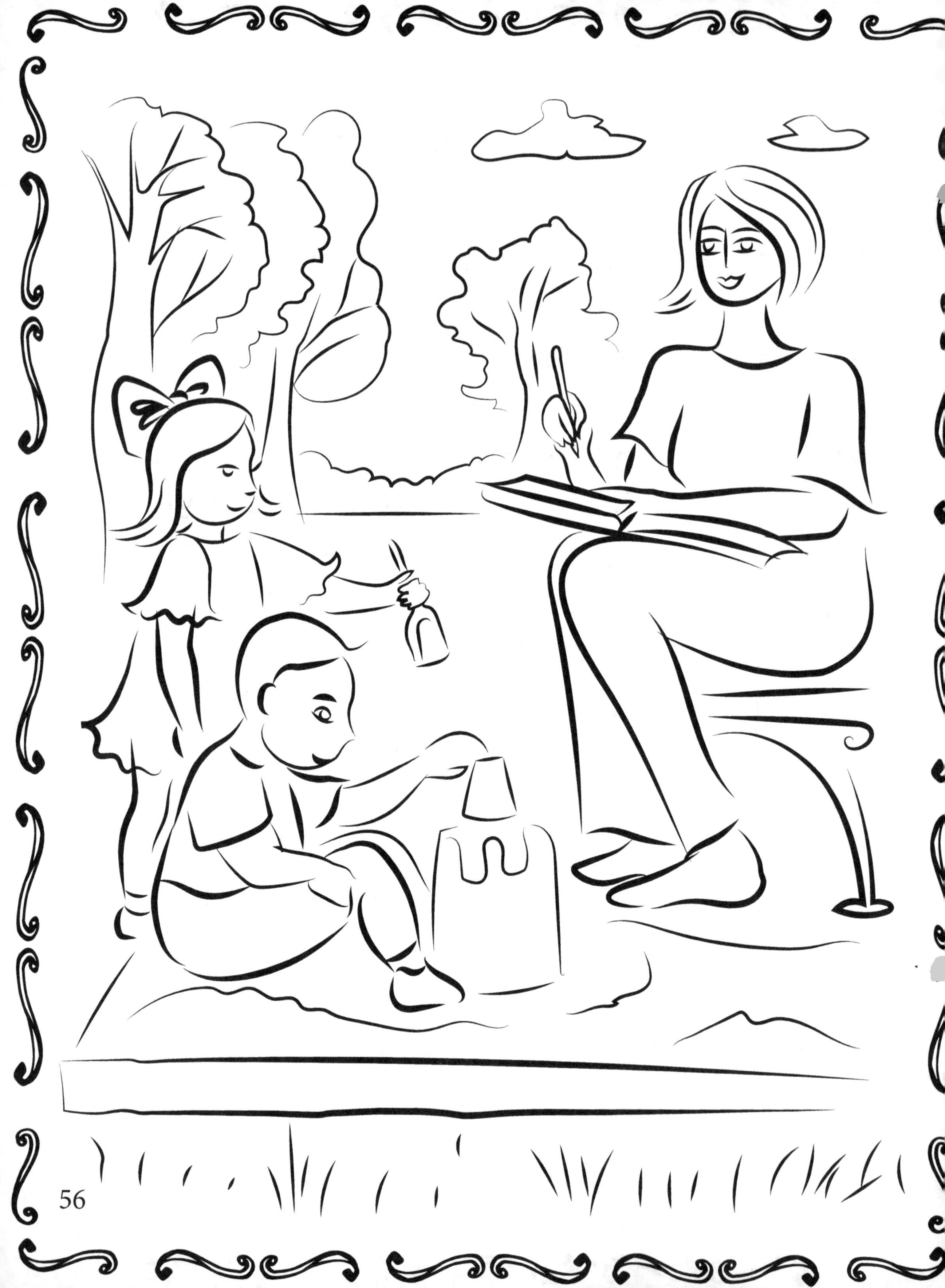

Final Note

Make sketching from life a regular practice.

Go to the park, or hang out with friends & family and draw them! You can also pose for yourself by using a full length or smaller mirror for portraits. Friends can pose for you via video chat, or you can view online videos and use them as a reference.

Finally, photo references are also acceptable and useful tools. After awhile, with lots of practice, you will be able to construct characters entirely out of your own imagination, or to combine made up characters with references.

Please remember to have fun - drawing is a joyful experience that will enrich your life in many positive ways for years to come!

Thank you so much for reading this book!
If you enjoyed it, please leave a review on Amazon!

Let's get drawing!

Collect All of Our "How To Draw" and more books.
Available at major retailers.

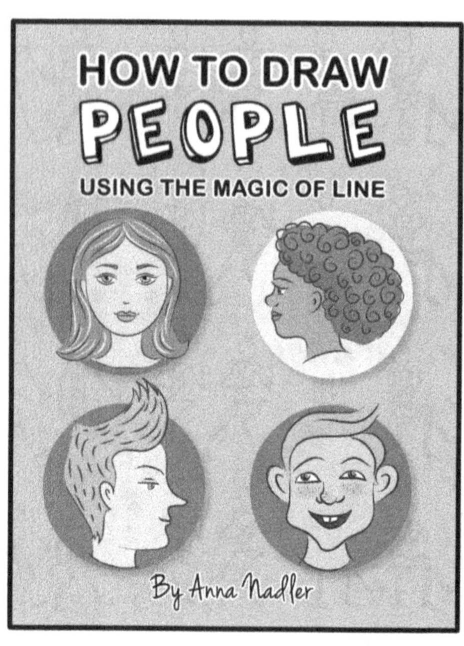

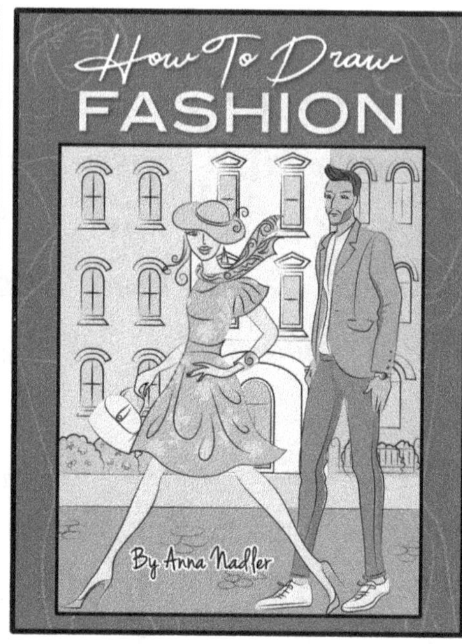

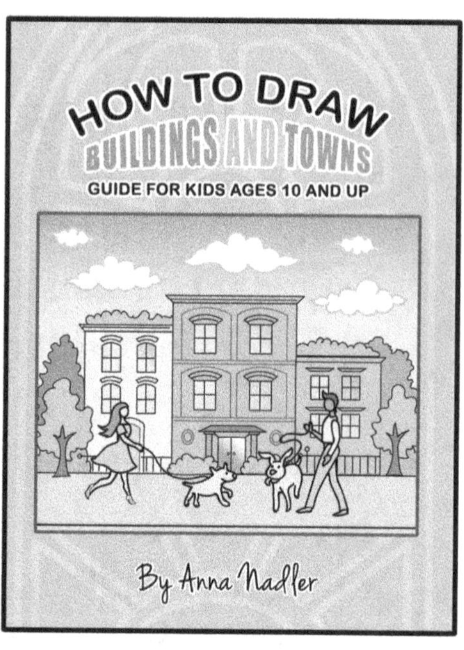

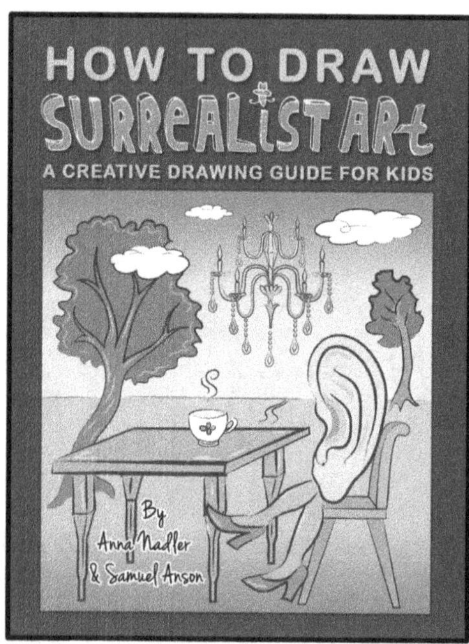

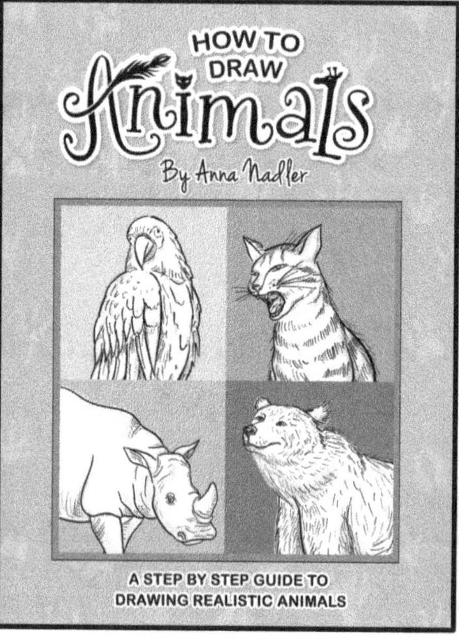

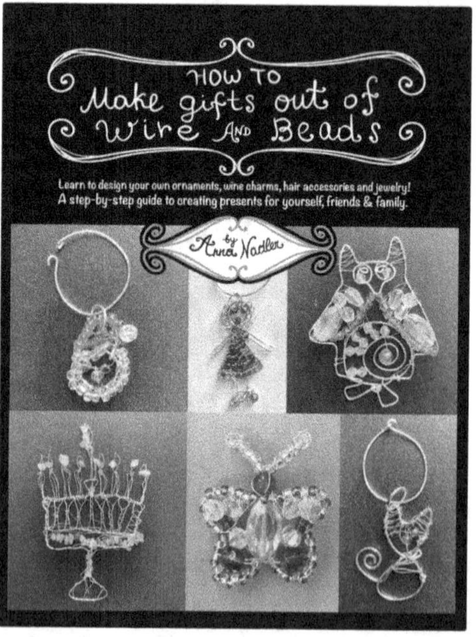

Thank you for getting
this book!

If you enjoyed it,
please
leave a review!

www.ingramcontent.com/pod-product-compliance
Lightning Source LLC
Chambersburg PA
CBHW081554100726
47818CB00106B/197